IMPLEMENTING AN AUTOMATED CIRCULATION SYSTEM

A How-To-Do-It Manual

KATHLEEN G. FOUTY

HOW-TO-DO-IT MANUALS
FOR LIBRARIANS

Number 43

NEAL-SCHUMAN PUBLISHERS, INC.
New York, London

Published by Neal-Schuman Publishers, Inc.
100 Varick Street
New York, NY 10013

Printed and bound in the United States of America

Library of Congress Cataloging-in-Publication Data

Fouty, Kathleen G.
    Implementing an automated circulation system : a how - to - do - it
manual / Kathleen G. Fouty.
        p.   cm. -- (A how-to-do-it manual ; no. 43)
    Includes bibliographical references (p .) and index .
    ISBN 1-55570-175-2
    1. Charging systems (Libraries) --Data processing .   I. Title.
II. Series: How-to-do-it manuals for libraries ; no. 43.
Z714.F68   1994
025.6 ' 0285--dc20   94-13008
                                                                CIP

TO GARY

CONTENTS

ACKNOWLEDGMENTS

Many individuals contributed, directly and indirectly, to this book, and I am grateful to them all. Special thanks, however, must go to the following individuals: the University of Minnesota Libraries Circulation Trainers who spent many long hours with me implementing our NOTIS Circulation Module in 1990/91 (Erik Biever, Sharon Born, Maggie Lindorfer, Christopher Loring, Nancy McCormick, Joan Mouchet, Suzanne Reisner, Becky Ringwelski, and David Zopfi-Jordan); the core of technical assistants for that same project who patiently provided me with a sound education in the finer details of automation (Connie Hendrick, Christina Meyer, Jon Howe, and Betsy Grzybek); my colleagues in the Science & Engineering Library, in particular Sandra Moline, for encouraging and supporting me in the writing of this book; my colleagues in other libraries who provided valuable input about their own automation projects (in particular, Pauline Iacono of the Ramsey County Public Libraries, Arlys Kempf now retired from the Madison, Wisconsin public schools, and Kristin Oberts of the 3M Company); and my husband, Gary Fouty, who was always there as a sounding board and who provided support and encouragement beyond measure during the more difficult stages of automation and writing.

PREFACE

Implementing an automated circulation system is a major undertaking for any library, whether circulation activities are being autoated for the first time, or one automated system is being exchanged for another. As libraries feel the pinch of tighter and tighter budgets, the luxury of bringing in an outside consultant to manage the implementation process is an unaffordable expense—libraries must rely on existing staff to manage this series of tasks. Often, the individual or individuals delegated this task have had little or no prior experience with a project of this magnitude and complexity, are offered little in the way of guidance, and learn "how-to-do-it" as they progress toward the project's completion.

INTENDED AUDIENCE

This book is intended to provide that missing guidance, alerting the reader in advance on "how-to-do-it" right, thereby reducing the potential for management faux pas and unpleasant surprises. Even though this how-to-do-it manual assumes no prior experience implementing an automated circulation system, most of the concepts offered are readily adapted to the implementation process for a second or even third generation system. The experienced practitioner may find it useful to review the entire implementation process, as presented in this manual, prior to undertaking a new project.

This manual focuses on the complex set of automation activities required by larger libraries, rather than the simpler processes that may be feasible in smaller, one-person libraries. Although specific strategies and techniques may vary according to the unique needs of each library, the concepts covered in this manual are fundamental to most automated circulation implementation projects, and can be adapted readily for application in academic, public, school, or special libraries.

TOPICS EXCLUDED

The library literature includes many resources that offer technical information about computer software and hardware. The literature also offers a number of fine publications that detail the automation process prior to implementation and provide guidance for such tasks as analyzing institutional needs, developing an RFP and system specifications/requirements, selecting system software, selecting hardware to support the system, and determining an appropriate communication link. These pre-implementation processes are beyond the scope of this how-to-do-it manual. Selected publications that do an excellent job of covering these topics are listed in the bibliography following Chapter 13.

TOPICS INCLUDED

The implementation process can be defined as the point at which the system software and hardware are tested and installed, bibliographic and patron data files are created to support the system, library policies and procedures are adapted as necessary, publicity and training are developed and delivered to library staff and users, and staffing and organizational issues raised by the system's installation are resolved. Each chapter will focus on one of these concepts, describing the array of tasks, issues and management decisions engendered in each. Although the arrangement of chapters follows a loose sequence in the course of implementing an automated circulation system, many of the tasks discussed will be managed *concurrently* rather than *sequentially*.

The strategies and techniques presented in this how-to-do-it manual have been developed as a result of synthesizing personal experience managing the implementation of an automated circulation system in one of the largest academic library systems in the United States, informal comments from others whose libraries have undergone this process, and a review and analysis of the library literature on the subject. The strategy and techniques described are ideals for which one might aim, rather than mandated approaches to be used and proscribed goals to reach. Ideals, tempered with a great deal of flexibility, have their place in the imperfect world of library automation. Adjustments to the order and comprehensiveness of the tasks presented in this book should be molded to fit a library's unique needs. Comparing the needs of one's own library to the comprehensive array of tasks detailed in this manual should serve as a convenient way to determine beforehand the probable magnitude of the project and its potential impact on the library and its user community. For the experienced manager implementing another generation of an automated circulation system, the manual will serve as a prompt to identify which tasks need to be revisited and to clarify what direction the project will take. For example, a library exchanging one system for another may already have its bibliographic records in machine-readable form and individual items barcoded. However, if that library is moving from a stand-alone circulation system toward an integrated automated system, the existing bibliographic records may need to be expanded with additional information. Or, the new system may require a different type of barcode, necessitating the initiation of another barcoding project prior to the system's implementation.

It is important to remember that while there is no one right way to implement an automated circulation system, there are an infinite number of wrong ways. The primary objective of this how-to-do-it manual is to provide guidance in avoiding the many pitfalls that can undermine the successful implementation of an automated circulation system.

1 INTRODUCTION

Over the past two decades, many libraries have taken advantage of improved library technology to convert their circulation activities from manual or batch processing systems to online, real-time systems. The decision to automate circulation activities has ranked high on most libraries' list of priorities. Automated systems impact almost every area of our lives today, from our commercial transactions with supermarkets, department stores, airlines, and banks, to our in-home or in-office word processing or file management, to our methods for communicating with friends, family, or colleagues. It is not unreasonable for library users to expect the library to be automated as well, offering them the same computerized efficiencies and accuracy they are accustomed to receiving in other areas of their lives.

Some libraries have yet to automate circulation activities, either as the first step in automating a variety of library functions or as another module within an integrated automated system. Other libraries usually contemplate the implementation of their next automated circulation system as a result of increased circulation activity that rendered the existing circulation system inadequate, demands from library staff and users for more sophisticated system features, or, the need for a move from a stand-alone circulation system to an integrated automated system. Since most automated systems have a life cycle of five to seven years, it may not be unusual to find automated libraries installing two new systems or major upgrades within 13 years of implementing the first.[1] Implementing automated circulation systems, whether they are first, second, or even third generation systems, will most likely continue to be a priority for libraries into the foreseeable future.

A BRIEF HISTORY OF CIRCULATION

Since their inception, libraries have utilized a wide variety of methods to record circulation transactions. During the course of the twentieth century, numerous means have been employed in an effort to streamline circulation activities (see Fig. 1-1). In particular, libraries have sought to ease the time-consuming, labor-intensive processes of recording and reviewing circulation information.

A wide array of diverse media were utilized prior to the advent of online automated systems, including ledgers with handwritten entries, cards that were handwritten, typed, embossed, edge-notched, or punched; multipart forms; punched paper tape; and microfilm.[2]

MANUAL CIRCULATION SYSTEMS

Manual recording of circulation transactions (i.e., noting in writing the title and/or call number of the item being borrowed, and the name and/or identification number of the individual to whom the item has been loaned) is the oldest process for recording circulation information—one that is still used in some libraries to circulate some or all of their collections. Handwritten ledgers, used for centuries to record book titles and borrowers' names, were replaced by handwritten or typed book cards that were created for each item owned by the library. When the item was loaned to a library user, the card was removed from the pocket in the back of the book and information about the user (name, address, identification number, etc.) was recorded on the card either in writing, by obtaining an imprint of an identification card, or some combination of both. The due date was stamped or written on the card. The card was then filed by whatever key element the library had selected for filing its circulation records (e.g., the item's call number, the individual's name, the due date, etc.). These large, meaningfully-arranged files replaced chronologically-arranged ledgers as the source for circulation information.

FROM MANUAL TO MECHANICAL CIRCULATION SYSTEMS

As early as the beginning of the twentieth century, numerous mechanical systems were developed in the quest for an even more efficient way for libraries to record and access library transactions. These mechanical systems included electromechanical systems, thermographic photographic images of library transaction records, and preprinted, prepunched cards.[3] Unfortunately, the mechanical systems had many of the same limitations as the manual systems, including:

1. limited information access points since creating duplicate records with additional access points for each item circulated was beyond most libraries' budgets,
2. difficult processes for determining the circulation status of specific items,
3. the potential for misfiled records, lost forever in larger files,

FIGURE 1-1   The Quest for the Perfect Circulation System

Era	System	Record Format
Prior to 1900	MANUAL	—Ledgers —Hand-written or Typed Cards
1900	MECHANICAL	—Punched Cards —Punched Paper Tape —Thermographic Photographic Images —Microfilm
1940	OFFLINE BATCH	—Machine-Readable Punched Cards —Machine-Readable Magnetic Tapes
1970	ONLINE, "REAL-TIME"	—Computerized Databases

4. cumbersome, ineffective blocking processes that made it impossible to block borrowing privileges for all but the most notoriously delinquent library users,
5. no means by which library users could be provided with a list of all the items they had currently charged,
6. no means by which library users could be informed of pending due dates, and
7. provision of only the most rudimentary statistics.

Although mechanical circulation systems were a step above hand-written, chronologically arranged records of library transactions, their limitations still hampered the efficiency of circulation staff in completing their day-to-day tasks, and severely limited the variety of services and information that staff were able to deliver to library users.

OFFLINE BATCH PROCESSING SYSTEMS

Significant improvements for recording circulation information began to be realized with the advent of offline batch processing systems. Automation of circulation activities began to take place in the 1940s as libraries installed offline batch processing systems, but very few of these systems were installed prior to the 1970s. The few that were installed during these three decades used either keypunch machines to produce machine-readable cards or key-to-tape technology to produce machine-readable tapes. These systems provided a quick and reliable way to collect circulation information, eliminated the manual filing of circulation records, and provided automatic printing of overdue notices; however, they did not provide access to circulation information until days after the information on the cards or tapes was read into the computer.[4] Although this first step in the automation of circulation activities proved to be a time-saver for libraries and allowed them to begin utilizing circulation staff in more productive ways, the nature of batch processing created a time-lag that diminished the currency and accuracy of the information available to library staff and users.

ONLINE REAL-TIME SYSTEMS

The mid-1970s ushered in a major boom in automation, as a result of computer hardware and software that could support time-shared interactive online activities becoming available.[5] As a result of these technological innovations, online real-time systems (the earliest prototypes developed by libraries) began to replace batch processing systems.[6] The major enhancement offered by these systems was their ability to record circulation information, such as a charge or discharge, instantaneously *and* allow library staff and users immediate access to the information. Online circulation systems also automatically and instantaneously provided information that was cumbersome, if not impossible, to elicit from manual or mechanical systems (for instance, an individual's eligibility for borrowing privileges). The automatic creation and "filing" of circulation transactions eliminated the possibility of misfiled records in larger files. The majority of automated circulation systems in use today are online systems that have been developed by commercial vendors.

In addition to allowing immediate access to up-to-date circulation information, online circulation systems also provide access to circulation information via numerous data elements related to either the library item (title, call number, item identification number) or its borrower (name, identification number). With the flexibility offered by online circulation systems, libraries are able to offer users services that were impossible with manual, mechanical, or batch processing systems, including such enhancements as notices announcing pending due dates and comprehensive lists of items charged to an individual library user. Online circulation systems have also allowed libraries to incorporate sophisticated features into automated circulation functions, including parameterization that allows individual libraries using the same system to set their own loan periods and fines, as well as security profiles that allow for varying degrees of authorization to perform circulation functions.[7] These systems allow for greater flexibility within a single library system by providing the means for multiple circulation points with multiple policies and procedures. In addition to facilitating circulation tasks and enhancing user services, online circulation systems also offer library management an impressive array of statistical data impossible to extract prior to the arrival of online circulation systems.

STAND-ALONE VS. INTEGRATED ONLINE CIRCULATION SYSTEMS

Over the past decade or two, online systems have evolved from simplistic single function systems that provided information about only one set of library functions (e.g., circulation, acquisitions, etc.), to complex integrated systems that deliver a well-rounded view within one system of the inter-relatedness of all library functions.[8]

Integrated online systems more closely represent the actual activities of the library, where one unit's processing of library material impacts material availability and the functioning of another unit. Integrated systems group a number of activities, (e.g., acquisitions, serials control, circulation and course reserves, the public-access catalog, bindery, and interlibrary loan) into one system using common commands and sharing common patron and item record databases. From a circulation standpoint, the most obvious benefit of an integrated system is the ability to track, throughout the library system and beyond, the movement of any particular item owned by the library. In addition, integrated systems provide access to information more comprehensive than any offered by a stand-alone system, thereby increasing the efficiency and service potential of library staff. Service with an integrated system transcends departmental or unit boundaries and provides a more comprehensive picture of the library's activities. These benefits have made integrated online systems the overwhelmingly popular choice today for library automation.

THE CURRENT STATE OF THE ART

There are many "bells and whistles" available with different automated circulation systems, but all should offer the same fundamental capabilities for basic circulation control. The system the library has purchased will probably include the following basic features:

1. efficient and effective charge and discharge functions;
2. the capability to record pertinent information about the user (name, address, identification number, etc.), and the ability to access this information whenever needed;
3. automatic maintenance of accurate, up-to-date circulation records;
4. information detailing the availability of individual library items, including when a library item will become available if currently unavailable;
5. information that allows for tracking an item's progress throughout various stages of its processing;
6. efficient hold and recall functions;
7. automatic production of overdue, recall, and hold notices, as well as bills;
8. automatic calculation of fines and re-calculation of outstanding totals after payment;
9. accommodation of multiple loan periods, fine levels, options defined by user category, and options defined by material type;
10. course reserves functions;
11. basic statistics that will assist with collection maintenance and staffing within the circulation unit; and,
12. the flexibility to handle, without major system modification, any dramatic increase in collection size, number of users, or number of transactions.[9]

The features listed above should operate accurately, consistently, efficiently, and thoroughly, with a convenience that renders their functioning transparent to library users. The information produced by the system should be reliable, and its provision timely. Also, these basic system features should, for the most part, function automatically and require minimal staff intervention. In addition to the basic features listed above, the system the library has purchased might include additional features, such as an array of batch-processed reports, or a flexibility that allows the library to determine user categories and loan periods, rather than accept the predetermined choices offered by the system.[10]

Given the volume and labor-intensive nature of circulation activities, the circulation control components in automated systems have received a great deal of attention and are generally the most intensively developed functions within a system.[11] Sophistication and flexibility are features that libraries now expect to find standard in automated circulation systems. As vendors of automated circulation systems become more attuned and responsive to these expectations, it's easier to purchase a system that meets many of the library's needs.

The benefits that will be realized by automating circulation activities are many and will include such improvements as a quicker and more efficient charge/discharge process; diminishing of routine, repetitive tasks; immediate, online access to information about individual items' circulation status; more accurate and precise inventory control; and, better identification of delinquent library users, allowing for a more consistent and uniform handling of policy infractions. However, there are some limitations to the improvements an automated system will provide. The new system will not prove to be the panacea for all library staff or user woes. Busy times will still occur and queues will still form at service desks. Inevitably, the system will experience down-time; no matter how infrequent or short, it will be an inconvenience. The information in the system will only be as accurate as the information that has been read into it. In addition, the system will only provide information about an item's circulation status, not whether or not it is actually on the shelf. The system has been designed for the routine, and will not deal well with exceptional situations. The system will require maintenance, and, in the short term, may be very expensive to implement and operate. Last but not least, the new system will produce its own unique, new set of problems. Although the benefits of a new or improved automated circulation system will still outweigh the limitations, enthusiasm should be tempered with a dose of reality prior to the system's implementation to avoid any disappointment.

PLANNING AND MANAGING THE IMPLEMENTATION PROJECT

Implementing the online circulation system is the culmination of the processes that analyze library needs, resulting in the selection of the system hardware and software. The implementation project will focus on the installation and activation of the system, the public relations and training programs that must be developed and delivered to library staff and users, and the evaluation of the system after it has become operational. This is an extremely critical phase of the automation process, and the success of the system, no matter how fine a system it is, is largely dependent on how well the implementation project is handled by the library.

IMPLEMENTATION TASKS

Whether the library is automating circulation activities for the first time or moving from one automated system to another, implementing an automated circulation system is a complex task involving many individuals. The process of taking a library through the implementation of a new system can be overwhelming if not properly planned. Tasks that will need attention during the implementation project include:

1. becoming familiar with and testing the system software and hardware;
2. bringing the library records (bibliographic, user, and circulation) up to par for use in the system;
3. evaluating library policies and procedures with respect to the new system, and, prior to the system becoming operational, revising and adjusting them if necessary;
4. compiling and distributing both system and library-specific documentation prior to the system becoming operational;
5. mounting training and public relations programs for both library staff and users;
6. addressing organizational issues that will be brought to the forefront by automation;
7. formalizing liaison activities between units within the library and between the library and other agencies or offices external to the library; and
8. establishing procedures to handle on-going tasks of policy and procedure review, training, and documentation de-

velopment and revision, as system changes and enhancements are implemented.

By reducing the overall implementation project to a series of manageable tasks, each with individual timelines, a system can be developed for dealing with the multitude of individuals who will participate in a seemingly infinite number of tasks as part of the implementation process. However, it is also critical that the project incorporate a good measure of flexibility in relation to any deadlines. Very few, if any, automation projects have been completed precisely within the original timeline. Because automation projects involve the participation of so many individuals, from library staff, to vendors, to laborers, and since the system itself can rarely be implemented by just loading the software and turning on the computer, major and minor delays are inevitable and some accommodation for such setbacks should be incorporated into the project's timeline. From drafting a procedure for the library's new circulation manual, to ordering hardware for the system, to creating any supplemental programming needed to make the system operational for the library, to processing a work order for electrical or telecommunications work, delays, both avoidable and unavoidable, will occur and must be taken into consideration.

STAFF INVOLVEMENT

Implementation of an automated circulation system does not happen automatically. A multitude of tasks need to be initiated, undertaken, and completed—some of them essential to the actual running of the system. In order to complete the tasks germane to the eight areas previously listed as comprising the implementation project, the activities and participation of numerous individuals must be coordinated. Within the library staff, front-line circulation staff, technical services staff, departmental libraries staff, data entry operators, trainers, typists, and clerks will all play a role in the system's implementation. In addition to the library staff, computer center or systems staff (such as programmers, software technicians, etc.), hardware technicians, electrical and communication technicians, non-library representatives from other offices or agencies within the same institution or company (such as personnel, payroll, identification card, or bursar's offices), and system vendor representatives will all play a part in the system's implementation.

Since the implementation project cannot be completed without a great deal of staff effort, it will require the investment of a significant amount of staff time. Whether that time commitment is spread among many staff members or delegated to a few key individuals is dependent on the needs and flexibility of the individual library. Even if a few key players are identified and given the major responsibility for the planning and tasks associated with the implementation project, all library staff will be involved in some way at different stages of the project. Front-line circulation staff will be needed to assist in evaluating library circulation policies and procedures and to assist with compiling data for table construction if the system is a table-driven system; technical services staff will be needed to assist in defining policies and procedures that relate to their functions (e.g., bindery issues, serials check-in issues, etc.); all library staff will need some degree of training on the system, from non-circulation staff who will need to know basic information about what the system will do and how it will behave to front-line circulation staff who will need to know how to complete their day-to-day tasks on the system. Of course, the assistance of library managers and administrators will also be required to support the implementation project and provide guidance on issues that require administrative decisions. Providing opportunities for broad staff involvement in the implementation project not only allows wider distribution of a heavy workload, but also promotes quicker staff acceptance of the new system. Gains are made on this front as staff acquire an increasing familiarity with the new system as well as the sense of ownership that participation fosters. Advance knowledge about how the system will actually work relieves fears of the unknown and eases psychological adjustment to the new system. It also eases staff into the realities of the system, reducing unrealistic expectations about the system and the potential for disappointment.[12] Knowledge of the system prior to its implementation, and staff support for that system, will go a long way in assuring the successful implementation of the system.

The implementation project will often seem labor-intensive, and the drain on the time of involved staff members will, at times, negatively impact the attention those staff members can devote to their primary responsibilities. Nonetheless, it is time well-spent. An investment of staff time in the short term to conduct a well-planned, efficient implementation project will save time and staff energy over the long term.

ON-GOING TASKS

Also to be considered is the never-ending nature of some tasks initially encountered in the implementation project. For instance, the need for training, public relations, and up-to-date documentation continues long after the automated circulation system has become operational. Continuing education through training, publicity that keeps library staff and users well-informed, and system and in-house documentation that reflects current policies and procedures will all need attention, to varying degrees, each time there is a change or enhancement to the system.

Success in implementing an automated system is never guaranteed. Even the best of plans can go awry when unforeseen circumstances intervene (e.g., the vendor files for bankruptcy, a shortcoming to the system thought minor prior to automation turns out to be a major problem once the system is operational, or the hardware purchased to support the system proves inadequate). However, the absence of any plans at all for the implementation of the new system will dramatically increase the possibility that the system will become a failure. A well-planned implementation project does not guarantee a successful automated circulation system, but it considerably reduces the risk of failure. In short, "automation is not for the impulsive."[13]

REFERENCES

1. Ellen Hoffman, "Managing Automation: A Process, Not a Project," *Library Hi Tech* 6 (1988): 46.
2. James E. Rush Associates, inc., *Circulation Control,* vol. 2 of *Library Systems Evaluation Guide* (Columbus, OH: Rush Associates, 1983): 20.
3. Richard W. Boss and Judy McQueen, "Automated Circulation Control Systems," *Library Technology Reports* 18 (March/April 1982): 128-9.
4. Ibid.
5. E. G. Fayen, "Automated Circulation Systems for Large Libraries," *Library Technology Reports* 22 (July/August 1986): 387.
6. Boss and McQueen, "Automated Circulation Control Systems," p. 131.
7. Richard W. Boss, *The Library Manager's Guide to Automation,* Third Edition (Boston, MA: G. K. Hall & Co, 1990): 31.
8. Joseph R. Matthews, "The Automated Circulation System Marketplace: Active and Heating Up," *Library Journal* 107 (February 1, 1982): 547.

9. See Richard W. Boss, *The Library Manager's Guide to Automation* (White Plains, NY: Knowledge Industry Publications, Inc., 1979): 29; Boss, *The Library Manager's Guide to Automation,* Third Edition, p. 7; and Rush, *Circulation Control,* pp. 21-2.

10. Paul Metz, "Circulation Systems: The Tinker Toys of Library Automation?" *Journal of Academic Librarianship* 13 (January 1988): 364d.

11. Matthews, "The Automated Circulation System Marketplace: Active and Heating Up," p. 235.

12. Danya Buck, "Bringing Up an Automated Circulation System: Staffing Needs," *Wilson Library Bulletin* 60 (March 1986): 31.

13. Boss, *The Library Manager's Guide to Automation,* Third Edition, p. 131.

2 LEADING THE IMPLEMENTATION PROJECT: THE PROJECT MANAGER

The first step in the process of implementing an automated circulation system will be to appoint a project manager. This individual will be responsible for leading and directing implementation project participants, and for coordinating and overseeing the many tasks associated with the implementation project (see Fig. 2-1). This appointment should be made by library administration as soon as possible once the library has decided to automate circulation activities or replace an existing automated system. At the very latest, this appointment should be made immediately after the automated circulation system has been selected. Given the magnitude and complexity of the implementation project, the project manager cannot be appointed too early.

REQUIRED QUALIFICATIONS INCLUDE. . .

In the final analysis, a variety of factors will determine the success or failure of the implementation of the new automated circulation system, including the acceptance or rejection of the new system by library staff and users. Without a doubt, though, the skill the project manager demonstrates in leading the implementation project toward completion will be one of the more critical determinants of the ultimate success or failure of the new system.

FIGURE 2-1   Project Manager, Automated Circulation Implementation

Position Description

The Best Library has implemented the Automated-Systems-R-Us library automation software. Automated-Systems-R-Us is an integrated system that supports acquisitions, book fund accounting, cataloging, serials records, and an online catalog. The Best Library is in the process of implementing automated circulation as part of the Automated-Systems-R-Us system. A full-time position is now available to current Best Library staff as Project Manager, Automated Circulation Implementation with the following responsibilities:

1. Create or convert data to construct system databases;
2. Gather data to define system parameters, such as loan periods, fines rates, and staff security profiles;
3. Test the system and its print products;
4. Coordinate the order and installation of system hardware;
5. Review current circulation policies and procedures for possible revision;
6. Create in-house system documentation;
7. Develop and deliver staff and user training programs;
8. Generate publicity for staff and users; and
9. Develop measurement techniques for post-implementation. system evaluation.

REQUIRED QUALIFICATIONS INCLUDE experience managing circulation services, preferably within the Best Library; knowledge of the Best Library's current circulation system; basic knowledge of the new technology and its applications in libraries; and experience working with different groups.

THE SUCCESSFUL CANDIDATE WILL ALSO SHOW EVIDENCE OF an ability to grasp the "big picture," attention to detail, ability to analyze problems, creativity, patience, stamina, and excellent communication skills.

Applications are due to Ms. Eloise Smith, Best Library Personnel Officer, 23 Best Library, by October 21.

The Best Library is an equal opportunity employer and specifically invites and encourages applications from women and minorities.

The successful implementation project will include a leader who possesses four basic qualifications:

1. experience managing circulation services,
2. knowledge of the current circulation system,
3. basic knowledge of the new technology, and
4. experience working with different groups of individuals.

EXPERIENCE MANAGING CIRCULATION SERVICES

Most likely, the role of project manager will fall to an individual already on the library staff. Ideally, this assignment will be given to an individual whose primary responsibilities already include the management of circulation services. The individual selected might be a manager directly responsible for a specific circulation unit or it might be someone who is responsible for a wider array of public services that includes circulation services. This is not a project to press on a staff member who has not had any management experience at all, believing it to be an opportune learning experience. Although a desire and innate ability to manage may be adequate qualifications for an inexperienced individual seeking management experience in a lower profile management position, a high profile position such as an automated system project manager requires that desire and innate ability be tempered with day-to-day management experience. Given the numerous activities that will require skillful coordination by the project manager, it is to the library's advantage to appoint an individual who has been able to acquire and refine, as a direct result of that individual's primary responsibilities, a wide range of management techniques. The project manager will, of necessity, be learning many new concepts and skills as the project progresses. Basic management skills should not be one of them.

The fundamental role of the project manager will be to coordinate the implementation of the automated circulation system by organizing and directing the participants, maintaining schedules for the completion of the numerous tasks associated with the implementation process, and ensuring that deadlines are met or adjusted without jeopardizing the success of the system implementation. An individual with prior management experience has already practiced and honed, on a day-to-day basis, the management skills required to complete projects of varying sizes and magnitude. The individual's record of success in handling these previous projects will indicate the likelihood of this individual's success managing a larger, more complex project such as the implementation of an automated circulation system.

KNOWLEDGE OF THE CURRENT CIRCULATION SYSTEM

Although it is useful, of course, for the project manager to have had some experience with front-line circulation activities, it is not essential since the project manager will rely heavily on assistance from members of the project team as well as the rest of the library staff. Among those individuals will be those whose primary responsibilities include circulation activities and the provision of circulation services.

However, it is important that the project manager have some understanding of the current circulation system and its procedures. While it is not absolutely necessary for the project manager to have a comprehensive grasp of every procedure and policy used in the current system, it is important that the project manager have a broad understanding of circulation activities and services, as well as the relationship of these activities and services to the library as a whole. Beyond this basic knowledge, the more the project manager understands about the current system, the more easily that individual will be able to interpret the new system in relation to the old one for the project participants. In particular, this understanding will enhance the project manager's ability to foster the infinite number of decisions that will lead to the development of the policies and procedures that will support system functions and allow library staff to deliver the best possible service to library users.

BASIC KNOWLEDGE OF THE NEW TECHNOLOGY
Although the project manager will also be able to rely on other individuals to advise and inform her or him regarding the technical elements inherent in the system and the implementation process, it is important for the project manager to have some knowledge of technology and the role it will play in implementing an automated circulation system. This does not necessarily mean that the project manager must be a "techie." Basically, the more comfortable the project manager is with computing concepts, the quicker that individual will be able to understand the finer points of the system and move the project toward completion. In addition, this technical know-how will allow the project manager to serve as a liaison between systems and non-systems project participants, as well as "translate" the system's mysteries into terms the non-systems project participants will understand.

Even if the individual selected for the role of project manager is, by happy coincidence, also an individual who is extremely knowledgeable about computers and computing, there still will be much to learn about the specifics of the new system as the implementation project proceeds.

EXPERIENCE WORKING WITH DIFFERENT GROUPS
The individual whose primary responsibilities have promoted contact with, and knowledge of, the political networks both within and outside of the library will be well-prepared to fill the role of

project manager. As the figurehead for the project, the project manager will be required to represent the implementation project and the new system in numerous forums and will serve as a liaison to a variety of groups both within and outside of the library. Some knowledge of these groups, including their role within the library, organization, or institution, will allow the project manager to utilize their support and/or services constructively throughout the implementation project.

THE SUCCESSFUL CANDIDATE'S PERSONAL CHARACTERISTICS

In addition to the four qualifications listed above, the following personal characteristics are desirable in a project manager.

AN ABILITY TO GRASP THE "BIG PICTURE"

The project manager must have an understanding of the needs of the library as a whole and be able to impart this "bigger picture" to the individuals who will take part in the system implementation project. This proves especially important when the project manager begins working with the technical systems staff contributing to the project. The project manager must understand, and be able to articulate, how the automated circulation system will fit into the library's overall program. This includes the ability to determine, within this framework, the library's goals and needs for the automated circulation system and the services it will allow the library to provide. Allowing the systems staff a glimpse of how their work will fit into the library's overall goals will provide clarification as well as rationale for the many tasks they will undertake. Likewise, the project manager should be able to convey to non-systems project participants the impact their decisions will have on the functioning of the automated system and the library. The project participants will be responsible for completing the detail work that will accompany the implementation of the new system. However, it will be up to the project manager to back up each decision made and each task completed with the overall framework of a broader perspective.

The project manager must be able to present the overall needs of the library without any biases or partiality for one unit or one viewpoint over another. This will not always be easy, especially if the project manager's primary responsibilities include representation of a specific circulation unit or division within the library. However, it is critical to the success of the project that the project manager be able to move beyond those ordinarily-acceptable biases in order to implement a library-wide system. Any conscious or unconscious attempt at favoritism or promotion of personal agendas will be resented by other project participants and may jeopardize the teamwork essential to the project's success. The project manager must always keep an open mind, listening carefully to all viewpoints on an issue before assisting the participants to reach a decision. Forcing individual or unit-based biases on a library-wide system may also be counterproductive to the smooth functioning of the system once it is activated. Solutions for solving whatever problem is at hand will originate from many sources—some of them unpredictable. For instance, in larger library systems it is especially important to guard against biases or assumptions when representatives from large, medium, and small library units are presenting their positions. Although the volume of activity in the larger circulation units does afford opportunities to generalize and form many accurate conclusions about optimal procedures or policies, these judgements are not infallible nor always appropriate for an automated environment or for units with a lower volume of activity. The processes the larger units have been using under the current circulation system may not be ideal, but may actually represent a compromise as the only solutions appropriate for handling a large amount of activity in that particular system. Perhaps a procedure that originated in a smaller circulation unit may be more appropriate in an automated environment.

This requirement that the project manager maintain an unbiased, open mind during the implementation project does not mean that this individual cannot present personal or unit-based viewpoints. It is appropriate for the project manager to participate during a group discussion, especially if the project manager's experience and knowledge would provide yet another viewpoint to inform the discussion. It is inappropriate, however, for the project manager to dominate the discussion, intimidate other participants, or autocratically impose decisions without entertaining alternative viewpoints. In promoting as bias-free an environment as possible for discussions and decision-making, it will also be important for the project manager to not allow any other individual or individuals within a group to utilize similar tactics.

ATTENTION TO DETAIL

It is inevitable that a project the size and magnitude of an automated circulation system implementation project will entail an infinite number of details. The tasks within the project, the data required for the system to function, the processes that must be analyzed and revised, all require an exceptional amount of detail work that can be irritating to an individual who prefers to manage in broad strokes. The project manager must be able to appreciate and contend with the endless barrage of complex details that will comprise the implementation process.

AN ABILITY TO ANALYZE PROBLEMS

Although they often may appear contrary to the precept, both manual and computerized systems operate using a fundamentally logical set of principles. There will be many times throughout the course of the implementation project that the project manager will be called on to trouble-shoot a problem or analyze a process, thoroughly examining every detail. An individual with analytical skills will find these situations a challenge rather than a burden.

CREATIVITY

Creativity serves to complement and balance analytical skills when implementing an automated system. Creative thinking is extremely useful when it is impossible to intuit the logic of a system.

Creativity is essential, as well, when dealing with the unknown. The new system cannot be fully known until it is actually in production on a day-to-day basis. Imagining how the system will perform in different situations, or what policies or procedures will capitalize on the system's strengths and minimize its weaknesses, plays a very important role in the process leading up to the system's actual implementation.

Two tasks associated with the implementation project, system publicity and training, also benefit from creative thought. A lively, innovative training program, and a clever advertising campaign will capture interest and promote the new system in a very positive light.

PATIENCE

For the many times deadlines are missed, project participants demonstrate human failings, and the system seems incomprehensible, the project manager will find it essential to have an infinite supply of patience.

STAMINA

Managing the implementation of an automated circulation system will subject the project manager to a high level of stress beginning the moment that individual accepts the assignment. Throughout the course of the project, the stress level will not deviate much from a peak high, thereby giving the project manager very little respite from its intensity. If anything, the stress will be heightened by whatever crisis is most pressing at the moment. Unfortunately, the project manager cannot expect to experience immediate relief once the system is finally activated. At this delicate juncture, the level of stress may even increase for a few weeks or even months as all the decisions made during the implementation process become visible to library staff and users, and the results of the planning process are put to the test in units throughout the library. To cope with a project that delivers stress of this magnitude and duration, the project manager must evince a good deal of stamina, both mental and physical.

EXCELLENT COMMUNICATION SKILLS

The project manager will be responsible for working with many individuals from a wide variety of backgrounds, and for communicating the progress of the project to an audience comprised of an even wider array of diverse individuals. The project manager must be able to communicate effectively to all of these individuals, utilizing a wide variety of formats and media to do so. The scope and content of the information delivered and the method used to communicate it will vary from the library director, to the system programmers, to the electrical technicians, to the library staff, and finally to the library users. A project manager with excellent communication skills will be able to meet the challenge of employing a variety of effective communication techniques.

In addition to communicating information during the course of the project, the project manager also must be able to sell the system to library staff and users. Promotional techniques will include but not be limited to whatever public relations program is developed to publicize the new system.

DEFINING THE ROLE OF THE PROJECT MANAGER

Just as important as the process of appointing a project manager is the need for library administration to clearly define the role the project manager will play in implementing the automated circulation system. Any limitations or constraints on the project manager's role should be identified at this initial stage. In addition, these discussions should include complete information about the fiscal resources the project manager will have available to implement the automated circulation system. The individual who has agreed to accept the role of project manager and library administration should be in complete agreement regarding the parameters of the project and the responsibilities of the project manager. Critical to the success of the implementation project will be the library administration's willingness to give the project manager the authority necessary to successfully complete the project.

Ideally, the project manager should be relieved temporarily of her or his primary responsibilities and reassigned to the implementation project on a full-time basis. To have the manager of such a large, important project trying to cope with divided responsibilities isn't beneficial to the project or to the individual's "home" unit. Both will suffer varying degrees of neglect, and the project manager will become too harried to do her or his best at either. In addition, the project manager who is too busy coping with two positions will lose some of the high-profile visibility that underscores the importance of the implementation project.

This is not to say it is impossible to manage the implementation project as an add-on to primary responsibilities, but it *will* diminish the energy and thoughtfulness that the project manager will be able to devote to the project. At best, some tasks may be forgotten or neglected as a result of a crowded schedule. At worst, the success of the implementation project, including staff acceptance of the system, may be jeopardized. The individual who has been temporarily relieved of primary responsibilities in order to assume a full-time position as project manager will be able to devote more time to the project. That individual will also be more accessible since his or her time and attention will not be divided between managing the project and managing other full-time responsibilities.

TASKS REQUIRED OF THE PROJECT MANAGER

The specific tasks required of the project manager will depend on a number of variables including the project manager's experience and abilities, the authority granted the position by library administration, the quantity and complexities of tasks that must be completed prior to the system's implementation, and whether the library is automating circulation functions for the first time or exchanging one system for another. Generally, however, the tasks will fall into four broad categories:

1. defining the project by detailing the tasks that must be completed prior to implementation of the system,
2. coordinating the scheduling of these tasks,
3. organizing and directing the activities of the project team and other ad hoc, task-oriented groups as they participate in these tasks, and
4. regularly communicating the progress of the implementation project to a variety of groups.

DEFINING THE IMPLEMENTATION PROJECT

First, and foremost, the project manager needs to analyze the project and determine exactly what tasks must be completed prior to the system becoming operational. This will include, but is not limited to the following steps:

a. Create or convert any data necessary to construct the system's databases.
b. Compile any data that must be entered into the system for local parameterization including loan periods, fines rates, and security authorizations for staff.
c. Test the system modules and print products.
d. Coordinate the ordering and installation of hardware to support the system.
e. Analyze, and revise as necessary, library policies and procedures that will be impacted by the implementation of the new system.
f. Create library-specific documentation to support the operation of the system.

g. Create a system training program and deliver it to library staff, as well as library users if appropriate.

h. Produce a publicity program that will target both library staff and users.

i. Evaluate the system subsequent to its implementation.

COORDINATING THE SCHEDULING OF IMPLEMENTATION TASKS

Once the tasks have been identified, goals need to be established and reasonable deadlines set for the completion of each task. Target dates for completing individual tasks should be set for the earliest date possible, incorporating enough flexibility to allow for adjustment of the schedule when deadlines slip. This flexibility will be especially critical when one or more tasks must be completed prior to undertaking subsequently scheduled tasks.

Directing the system's installation includes coordinating the many variables associated with installing the system software and hardware. A comprehensive plan of action will be needed for the installation of the system software, from its initial installation and testing, to the first day of its actual operation within the library. Any data that will need to be entered into the system to supply its databases or provide local parameterization will need to be gathered, input, and tested for accuracy. A detailed testing script will need to be developed to test each function within the system's application software as well as the print and batch products the system will produce. A schedule should be identified for moving the tested, bug-free files and functions from the experimental testing region of the system into the production region where they will be used for day-to-day operation.

Prior to the installation of the system's hardware, the number of staff workstations and their placement within the library will need to be identified. In conjunction with this step, it will also be necessary to identify all of the telecommunications and electrical wiring needed to make each workstation a functional part of the system. Coordinate hardware installation with the installation of the system software. The system hardware should be tested as thoroughly as the system software.

Problems, major and minor, are inevitable when installing the system software and hardware. The project manager will need to be available as a resource person for the computer programmers, technicians, and library staff, serving as a liaison between the individuals encountering the problem and the experts who can identify a solution.

In addition to scheduling tasks for the actual implementation of the system, the project manager will also need to coordinate tasks that will result directly from the implementation of a new circulation system. There will be a myriad assortment of tasks associated with the analysis and revision of current library policies and procedures, development of staff and user training programs, promotion of the system to library staff and users, and creation of system and library-specific documentation.

COMMUNICATING THE PROGRESS OF THE PROJECT

It should be clear to all participants in the project, as well as to library staff who are not participating directly in the project, exactly who is leading the implementation of the new system and who may be contacted with questions. The project manager should be able to sustain a high degree of visibility. This will be mandated somewhat by the degree of involvement required, but will also be a function of communication techniques selected for keeping both project participants and non-participants up-to-date on the progress of the project. As mentioned earlier, the project manager will need to have an assortment of excellent communication skills to manage this aspect of the implementation project.

Through regular oral or written communications detailing progress, the project manager provides a high profile that serves a number of purposes. Communication ensures that everyone knows how the project is progressing, and what decisions and discussions are preceding the implementation of the system. It can be useful to allow staff members who are not participating in the implementation project a chance to review project participants' discussions and decisions. It may be easier for individuals not closely involved in the project to identify potential problems. Identifying potential problems and correcting them at this initial stage will cause fewer headaches and embarrassment than contending with actual problems once the system has become operational. Regular communication also provides a means of delivering easily-digested "sound-bites" of information about the system that will prepare the audience for the day the system becomes operational, but won't overwhelm them with too much information at once. Regular communication regarding the project's process plays a vital role in ensuring that the importance and magnitude of the project is not underestimated by anyone within or outside of the library.

Progress reports will need to be delivered to a number of groups and individuals in a variety of formats. The library administration and staff should be targeted, as should library users, formally appointed library committees or boards, and individuals in other offices or agencies who might be interested in or impacted by the system's implementation. Announcements or articles in newsletters or newspapers, publication of the minutes or summaries of the project team's meetings, and verbal presentations by the project manager to a variety of groups can all be used to announce completed tasks, unexpected problems, and the overall progress of the project.

3 WORKING WITH PROJECT PARTICIPANTS

Once the project has been analyzed, with tasks identified and deadlines set, the project manager is responsible for organizing and directing the completion of these tasks by utilizing assistance and support from a variety of groups and individuals (see Fig. 3-1). As the figurehead for the implementation project, the project manager will rely on two groups for primary support throughout the project: 1) the *members of the project team* who will assist the project manager with many of the tasks that must be completed prior to the new automated circulation system becoming operational (such as training, publicity, documentation, etc.), and 2) the *technical staff* who will be responsible for the installation and fine-tuning of the software that will run the new system. In addition, the project manager will seek support and assistance from other individuals and groups, including the library director, library administrators and managers, and ad hoc groups formed to tackle specific implementation tasks.

THE PROJECT TEAM

The project team will consist of a small group of individuals, preferably ten or less, who have been selected to assist the project manager throughout the course of the project. The project team will be a key group in the implementation of the new system, sharing with the project manager the tasks that must be completed and the decisions that must be made prior to the new system becoming operational. The project manager, with the assistance of the project team, will serve as the focal point for guiding the implementation of the new system. As with the project manager, the project team should be appointed as early in the implementation process as possible.

Prior to making any appointments to the project team, library administration, in consultation with the project manager, will need to decide what role will be played by the project team in the course of implementing the new system. The role of the project team should complement and support that of the project manager. It should be clearly defined in a formal, written charge that is distributed to all team members, the project manager, and any other individuals or groups who may be effected by the project team's activities. Formalization of the project team's anticipated activities is especially critical when dealing with the library's internal politics. Turf battles are less likely to develop if all are in agreement over the delegation of specific responsibilities.

Will the project team be responsible for all implementation tasks except those concerning policy or procedure decisions? *Or,* will the project team be responsible for all implementation tasks, including those that require developing procedures and recommending policies for use with the new system? If no other group, such as a circulation advisory group, exists to perform these tasks, they will fall to the project team by default. If, however, the library has a circulation advisory group, a decision must be made as to how the two groups will interact. It will be difficult to divide implementation tasks and policy/procedure decision-making between the two groups. These areas are often interdependent when implementing an automated circulation system, and discussion of one often raises elements of the other. If the project team will be responsible for undertaking system tasks, and the advisory group takes responsibility for making procedural and policy decisions, duplication of effort will occur as the two groups work separately on their assigned responsibilities. In addition, an extra bureaucratic layer will be added to the implementation project. Any recommendations concerning policies or procedures that arise during the course of the project team's discussions will require discussion and approval by the advisory group. This additional step in the approval process will necessitate factoring in additional time for the overall implementation project. One way to overcome the cumbersome nature of this split responsibility is to include significant representation from the advisory group on the project team. Doing so will allow the project team to either eliminate this additional bureaucratic layer and forward policy/procedural recommendations directly to library administration for approval, or quickly pass them through an advisory group that has largely participated in their formation.

SELECTING INDIVIDUALS FOR THE PROJECT TEAM
Bearing in mind what responsibilities have been defined for the project team, library administration and the project manager need to agree on how team members will be selected (for instance, rep-

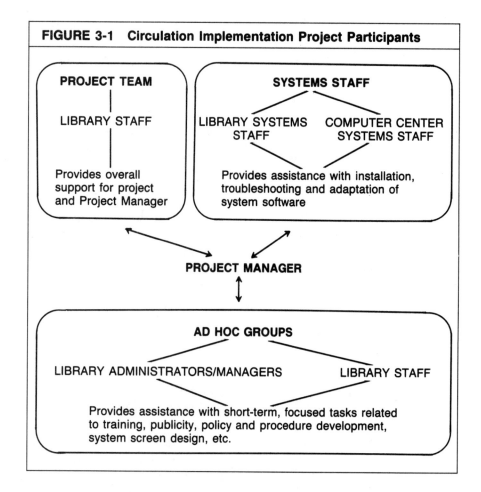

FIGURE 3-1 Circulation Implementation Project Participants

resentatives from different library units, representatives from an existing circulation advisory group, individuals with technical skills, individuals with front-line circulation responsibilities, etc.), and by whom (by the project manager, the administration, or both). The project team should be large enough to include adequate representation for groups of staff whose jobs will be effected by the automated system, but not so large as to become unmanageable. The optimal number of individuals comprising the project team will depend on the size and complexity of the library, but should generally range from five to ten members. A data processing professional also may be included as a full member of the team, or as an ex-officio member who participates when issues arise needing input from such an expert.

The definition of what is representative will depend a great deal on the internal politics of the library, however, representatives from circulation services and technical services should comprise the backbone of the team's membership since these two groups have the largest stake in the new system. Even though they will use it differently, both technical services and circulation services staff will be the heaviest users of the new automated circulation system once it is operational, and will rely on it to perform many of their daily tasks.

Once representative areas have been defined, individuals within those areas can be identified for the project team. Required qualifications for a team member will include enough experience with the current circulation system to acquire a comprehensive understanding of how the current system works as well as knowledge of the policies and procedures that support it. Personal characteristics that include flexibility, adaptability, creativity, and vision will enable the individual to assist constructively with the transition from one system to another. Technical expertise is a desirable qualification, since team members who understand state-of-the-art technology will prove useful in deciphering some of the finer points of the system's operation. However, this should not take precedence over the aforementioned experience and personal qualifications. Technologically knowledgeable individuals who know little about the current system, or who are bound by the current way of doing business and find it difficult to justify a policy or procedure change may not be productive or happy team members. They may find it especially difficult to be constructive team members when the group undertakes the multitude of implementation tasks that have little to do with the technicalities of system operation, and much to do with change in the way the library will do business.

RELEASE TIME FOR MEMBERS OF THE PROJECT TEAM
It is essential that a clear understanding be reached at this initial stage concerning release time for staff members participating as members of the project team. This understanding must be shared by library administration, the project manager, members of the project team, and supervisors of project team members. Release time can become a very sticky issue during the course of the project as tasks and deadlines become more pressing and decrease the time project team members can devote to their primary responsibilities. Although it is essential to include any mention of release time in the formal, written charge to the project team, it is not enough to have in writing a statement that team members will be granted a certain percentage release time to work on the project.

At the outset of the project, staffing alternatives or a rearrangement of responsibilities must be available to the individual's home unit so that neither the participating staff members nor their home units suffer from the individual's participation in the implementation project. If this is not resolved at the beginning of the project, team members will feel unfairly pressed for time as tasks mount, and the quality of the system's implementation may be diminished. Either the team's workload will be unfairly distributed among individual members, building resentment among team members, or essential tasks will remain uncompleted well beyond deadlines, delaying the implementation and fostering the perception that the implementation, or even the system, is not successful. The same holds true for the individual's home unit. The individual's normal workload may arbitrarily fall to resentful staff in the home unit, or these duties will be neglected to the point that the home unit, other units within the library, or library users will suffer. Like the project manager, all members of the implementation team should be able to devote their best energies to the project.

WORKING WITH THE PROJECT TEAM

Although the project manager is ultimately responsible for the success or failure of the implementation project, the project team plays a very important role as the project manager's key tool in the implementation process. The project team assists the project manager with developing the timeline for the project and also helps generate ideas for accomplishing the individual tasks associated with the implementation project. Additional responsibilities for the project team will include active support for the project and the new automated circulation system, and assistance with and/or full responsibility for specific tasks associated with the implementation project.

Shortly after the appointment of the project team, the project manager should share with the group the timeline for the implementation project, including an explanation of specific tasks and their deadlines. There should be a full discussion of the timeline, including identification of any potential problems that may indicate a revision of specific deadlines. After the project manager and project team agree on a final timeline for the project, the project manager should begin to steer the project team through the various tasks. The project manager will be responsible for distributing tasks among project team members, monitoring progress, and gently directing and providing guidance on a day-to-day basis.

Once the project manager and the project team begin their activities, it is important that discussions, recommendations, and decisions be documented. The best way to ensure adequate documentation, and to make sure that all important discussions and decisions are recorded and reported, is to write up formal minutes for each meeting of the project team. No one likes to take minutes, or worse, write them up after the meeting, but this is an extremely helpful method for documenting discussions and decisions related to the implementation process. If the project manager can rely on one or more members of the group to be vigilant and record the level of detail necessary, this task may be delegated or rotated among project team members. These records of the project's movement forward should be as widely disseminated as possible so that there are no surprises once the system is operational. Even though the project team may have been formed as a representative body, individuals within the group may not always communicate the progress of the implementation project to their colleagues. Routing the minutes to library administrators and staff whose jobs will be affected by the system will help address this gap. If the library has a newsletter in which committee minutes are routinely published, minutes of the project team's meetings would be good to add to the list. By distributing the project team's minutes as widely as possible to reach the largest possible audience, all effected staff will be apprised of what decisions are being made and the rationale for each decision. Also, any red flags or erroneous conclusions are more easily corrected when spotted early in the implementation process.

In addition, although the project team will have a written charge, issues will arise for which responsibility is unclear. If an issue or task confronting the project team appears to overlap the responsibilities of another group, such as library administration or a circulation advisory group, the wise project manager will refer the issue or task to library administration and allow that group to resolve the issue or assign responsibility for the task. Ignoring these finer points by allowing the project team to forge ahead and tackle the issue or task head-on may alienate or offend other groups who feel they have a vested interest or responsibility in the matter. These groups may not be as willing to participate or support the implementation project or system if they feel undermined by the process or unjustly excluded.

The project manager, when working with the project team, will need to call on her or his management and interpersonal skills throughout the duration of the project. The project manager must be a diplomat, but not to the point of coddling the group or individual members within the group. The project manager needs to take into account individual personalities and varying levels of comfort in working with this overwhelmingly complicated, unknown system, and make adjustments in task assignments when necessary. However, the project manager should avoid falling into the trap of trying to do everything simply because others have expressed discomfort about the time or skill they will be able to bring to a specific task. Tactics ranging from gentle prodding to forceful pep talks will need to be employed at various times. If the groups' original charge has indicated the availability of release time for project activities, individuals may need to be reminded of this provision in their original appointment to the group. They may also need to be reminded that *all* members of the project team are busy individuals, and one of the premises for creating the project team was to share the burden imposed by the many tasks inherent in the implementation project. Team effort means that members work together rather than individually find excuses to divert the workload. Also, it is important to point out that no one is truly experienced or a system expert at this stage of the system's implementation. Everyone involved in the implementation project will have much to learn over the course of the project. Progress in this area often goes unrecognized in the face of the multitude of system details that have yet to be learned or mastered. To emphasize how much progress members of the project team are making in this area, it is useful to point out to the group at various points during the project just how much they have already learned about the system.

THE TECHNICAL EXPERTS: THE SYSTEMS STAFF

To varying degrees and depending on the system the library has selected, the project manager will need to interact with the staff who are responsible for installing, trouble-shooting, and adapting the software for the new automated circulation system. Most institutions will have purchased either turnkey systems or vendor-supplied software. A turnkey system will require the least amount of effort to implement, as it comes pre-packaged without any need for additional programming. Vendor-supplied software will require more fine-tuning since programs may need to be adapted to suit the specific needs of the library. Depending on the staffing resources available in the library, and the amount of work needed to install and maintain the system, the library will either rely on its own staff for these technical systems tasks, or will to turn to an external resource for assistance, such as the computer center systems staff within the agency, organization, or institution of which the library is a part. Ideally, these systems experts will be dedicated solely to assisting the library with this project, and will be housed within the library.

No matter who comprises the systems staff, the project manager will need to work closely with these individuals to thoroughly test the system functions provided by the application software, and the print and batch products generated by the system; assist with the development of any additional programming required by the library to adapt the system to its specialized needs; and serve as the primary resource person for questions that will arise as the systems staff troubleshoot and debug the system software.

THE LIBRARY'S SYSTEMS STAFF

The library that includes a fully staffed systems office is fortunate indeed. These system experts may be individuals on the library staff who have demonstrated an aptitude for technology and automation, individuals with computer science backgrounds and training who have been specially hired as systems staff, or a combination of the two. Depending on the size of the staff, the extent to which the library has automated, and the complexities demanded by the new automated circulation system, the scope of responsibilities assumed by the systems staff during the implementation of the new system may vary. Generally, the library systems office will assume the following responsibilities:

1. technical support to implement the system, including coordinating compatible hardware with the system software, running system jobs, and coordinating a maintenance contract,
2. initial training on newly-acquired systems or modules, and
3. development or acquisition of system documentation.[1]

If the staff in the systems office includes individuals who have had experience working in a library or who have been trained as professional librarians, the project manager will have the good fortune of working with systems staff who have a good understanding of libraries. If these individuals have been culled from the library staff, the systems office will have an even more specific understanding of how this particular library works. With a systems staff comprised of individuals trained in computer science, but lacking any training or experience in libraries or librarianship, there is a greater challenge for the meeting of minds over a common system.

THE COMPUTER CENTER SYSTEMS STAFF

The library without its own in-house systems staff will rely on its parent agency, organization, or institution's computer center systems staff for technical support implementing the new automated circulation system. Even if the library organization includes an in-house systems staff, the organization's or institution's computer center systems staff may be used if the new system will run on a large micro- or mainframe computer operated by the computing center. In particular, this is not an uncommon situation in academic libraries. As more academic libraries install their automated systems on campus computers rather than library computers, more working collaborations are being established between staff in libraries and campus computing centers.[2]

The project manager will find the computer center systems staff to be invaluable. A good automated circulation system consists of numerous programs with many thousands of lines of codes.[3] The complexity of such a program provides a challenge for the project manager and the computer center systems staff as they work toward implementing a system that will process circulation information efficiently and accurately. In addition to de-mystifying computers and computer technology, the computer center systems staff can provide assistance installing the system software, testing and debugging the system, coding any data for system entry, and the day-to-day maintenance of the system once it has been activated.[4] Also, if the library plans to interface the automated circulation system with other databases or systems within the organization or institution, such as the registration and payroll databases or the bursars office's system, the computer center systems staff will be in a position to help the library establish these interfaces as quickly and efficiently as possible.

Many similarities exist between the services provided by computer centers and libraries. Both departments are often organized in a similar fashion. However, computer centers' organizational structures are less hierarchical than libraries' and an individual's role within the computer center's organizational structure is not dictated by their position within a formal structure but by the technical expertise that individual has acquired.[5] This fundamental difference in organizational structures, coupled with the different terminology employed by computer center staff, can create communication challenges when library staff and computer center systems staff are required to work together on a project.

> In large projects where individuals from the two different organizations must work together, differences in "culture" can lead to misunderstandings and friction. If "proper," library-type communication channels aren't used by computing center staff, library staff may misunderstand intentions and feel that they aren't being kept informed. For their part, computing center staff may feel that the library staff at times are bureaucratic, inflexible, and unresponsive.[6]

> Developing a common understanding is a challenge because librarians and programmers have different values and vocabularies.[7]

One of the keys to avoiding these "culture clashes" as much as possible is for the project manager and the computer center systems staff to interact and communicate as much as possible. By working together on a daily basis, undertaking and resolving problems both large and small, each comes to understand better the other's language and working environment. Throughout the course of the project, the project manager must take seriously the responsibility to fully explain the library's perspective for specific situations. Giving the computer center systems staff as many peeks as possible into the world of the library, its operations, and its user demands provides a better basis for formulating an understanding of the library and its automated system needs. Similarly, it is useful for the project manager to ask questions of the computer center systems staff and show a sincere interest in these individuals and their work as it relates to the implementation of the automated circulation system. As staff in the library and computer center each gain a better understanding of the other's role, expertise, and responsibilities, more time is spent by project participants productively coping with the system and its vagaries and less energy is wasted resolving petty annoyances. In short, both the project manager and the computer center systems staff need to achieve an understanding of each other's work environment and reach compromises that are comfortable and promote a productive working relationship.[8]

In general, it is not unreasonable for the project manager to expect the computer center systems staff to provide service that embodies "stability, reliability, responsiveness, sensitivity, the establishment of communication protocols, and a focus on production."[9] By the same token, it is not unreasonable for the computer center systems staff to expect the same from the project manager. If this is the first project to bring the computer center and library staff together, a working agreement might be detailed and agreed on prior to beginning work on the project. For instance, the library might draft a set of guidelines that clearly defines for the computer center systems staff the library's service expectations. After sharing the guidelines and modifying them to both parties' satisfaction, a written memorandum of agreement may be finalized. The contents of a memorandum of agreement might include the following:

1. Both the hardware and the software of the automated circulation system should be available during a schedule agreed on by both the library and computer center systems staff.
2. Both the library and computer center systems staff should approve, in advance, any changes to that schedule.
3. Both the library and computer center systems staff should approve, in advance, any modifications to the system software.
4. The computer center systems staff should involve library staff in plans to upgrade system hardware.
5. The computer center systems staff should alert the library staff well in advance when a service or product cannot be delivered at the promised time. The two groups should then agree on a new delivery date or deadline.[10]

Keeping the lines of communication open between the library and the computer center systems staff is the responsibility of many individuals from both areas. However, one individual within the library should be designated as the primary liaison to the computer center systems staff. If the library has its own systems office, a staff member from that unit may assume this responsibility. Or, primary responsibility for interacting with the computer center systems staff may rest with the project manager. No matter who is assigned this role, it is incumbent on the library representative to make sure any elements of the implementation plan involving computer center systems staff are communicated clearly to those individuals. Implementation tasks assumed by the computer center systems staff should be completed with as much advising from library staff as the computer center systems staff requests. By maintaining a constant flow of communication and combining it with a desire to understand both the technicalities of the system and the complexities of the computer center systems staff's role in the process, the library may be lucky enough to establish a productive working relationship that will yield benefits even after the system has been activated.

ADDITIONAL PROJECT PARTICIPANTS

As mentioned earlier, the implementation of an automated circulation system is a massive task that will require the efforts of more than just the project manager, the project team, and systems staff. In addition to these primary three, other groups or individuals who will be instrumental, to varying degrees, in the implementation of the new automated circulation system will include:

1. the library director and administration,
2. staff whose jobs will be directly impacted by the elimination of the current system and/or the implementation of the new system,
3. managers in areas where staff will be directly effected by the system's implementation, and
4. staff who may not be directly effected by the system's implementation, but who have experience that would be beneficial to draw on.

Involvement of library staff in the implementation project will be broadened by supplementing the project team with a number of ad hoc, task-oriented groups throughout the course of the project. At different stages of the project, different types of committees or working groups will need to be formed and assorted individuals consulted. Assigning additional staff members as needed to short-term, task-focused groups will allow the project manager to take advantage of many areas of staff expertise throughout the course of the implementation project and distribute the workload more evenly.

The need for these additional task-oriented groups will evolve as the project progresses. Groups may be formed to assist with training, publicity, policy and procedure development, or system screen design. Forming these groups on an as-needed basis allows the project manager an opportunity to gather together staff with special skills to work on projects that benefit from these particular skills. Some of these ad hoc groups will be short-lived and serve a single purpose, for instance, a group of individuals working in fines units might be formed to draft procedures for creating bills using the features provided by the new automated circulation system. Other groups might be formed to serve needs that are more complex and long-term. If such a committee doesn't already exist, library administration will probably want to appoint a representative body of staff who will be using the circulation system and who will be charged to advise library administration on circulation policies and procedures during and after the system's implementation.

All groups should have their specific charges in writing so there is no confusion or misunderstanding as to exactly what each group will be doing. The written charge can range from a formal charge to the group on letterhead stationary from the library director to an informal memo drafted by the project manager and sent to all members of the ad hoc group via electronic mail. The formality of the group's written charge will depend on how long-term or large a responsibility is being assigned.

Even though the prospect of creating additional committees or working groups to support the implementation of the new automated circulation system may raise concerns about yet more staff time diverted from primary responsibilities, the benefits of this supplemental staff involvement in the implementation project become more obvious as the project proceeds. Charged with solving a specific set of problems or completing one or more tasks related to the system's implementation, individuals assigned these tasks as a result of their special expertise or experience complete their activities more quickly, and perhaps with more insight, than individuals who lack the necessary expertise. Staff involvement in the implementation project is a critical step in developing staff interest and support for the new system. Allowing staff to take part in the implementation project in a way that underscores these individuals' importance to the accurate, efficient functioning of the system promotes a sense of ownership of the new system while strengthening staff support for that system. It also bears repeating that anyone who participates in the implementation project cannot help but acquire some knowledge, perhaps expert knowledge, of the new system. Having as many knowledgeable individuals as possible on staff prior to system start-up will provide a broader, more dispersed base of staff members who will be able to serve as resources for system information and troubleshooting. The more knowledgeable individuals there are scattered throughout the library, the more readily answers can be supplied to questions that arise once the system is operational.

REFERENCES

1. Association of Research Libraries, Systems and Procedures Exchange Center, *Automated Library Systems in ARL Libraries,* SPEC Kit #126 (Washington, D.C.: Association of Research Libraries, Office of Management Studies, Systems and Procedures Exchange Center, July-August 1986): 2.
2. Paul Metz, "Circulation Systems: The Tinker Toys of Library Systems," *Journal of Academic Librarianship* 13 (January 1988): 364a.
3. Ibid., p. 356c.
4. John Corbin, *Developing Computer-Based Library Systems* (Phoenix, AZ: Oryx Press, 1981): 36-37.
5. Metz, "Circulation Systems: The Tinker Toys of Library Systems," p. 364a.
6. Ibid., p. 364b.
7. Ellen Hoffman, "Managing Automation: A Process, Not a Project," *Library Hi Tech* 6 (1988): 48.
8. Metz, "Circulation Systems: The Tinker Toys of Library Systems," p. 364b.
9. Ibid.
10. Ibid.

4 INSTALLING THE APPLICATION SOFTWARE

As soon as the new automated circulation system has been selected, key participants in the implementation project (e.g., the project manager, the project team, and the systems staff) should begin reviewing documentation for the system, attending any user group meetings, establishing contacts with other libraries using the same system, and conducting site visits to see how the system operates in day-to-day use. Each contact with another user of the same automated circulation system will provide a different perspective on the system's limitations and capabilities. Combining these real-world perspectives and observations with the factual content of the system documentation will provide project participants a comprehensive introduction to both major and minor features of the system. This will also provide a sound base of knowledge which can be used to meet the challenges that will arise in the initial phase of system implementation (e.g., during the installation, testing, and modification of system software).

THE SOFTWARE

What functions should the software for an automated circulation system provide? At its most basic level, the application software should be able to process the linking and unlinking of item and patron records as library users borrow and return library materials. However, additional features are desirable in an automated circulation system. Most automated circulation systems will include most or all of the following features:

- the immediate updating of files to reflect borrowed, renewed, or returned items;
- the availability of information detailing an item's location and current circulation status;
- the ability to process renewals;

- the provision of lists of charged materials by individual borrower;
- the detection of an excessive number of items charged to an individual borrower;
- the automatic calculation of fines that also allows for any necessary adjustments by library staff;
- the automatic production of overdue and recall notices, and bills;
- the ability to block a delinquent patron's borrowing privileges;
- the capability to "flag" certain item records so that important messages will alert staff that items being discharged need special treatment instead of routine re-shelving; and
- the provision of statistically-based management reports.[1]

As evidenced by this list of features, automated circulation systems can perform many complicated circulation functions. The processes used to complete such activities are largely transparent to the users of these systems. However, this smooth operation is not managed without some effort, especially if the automated circulation system selected is not a turnkey system. The software that supports these features includes a complex set of programs that will require the efforts of numerous individuals, primarily systems/programming experts, to install and maintain. These tasks may become even more complicated if the application software provides opportunities for modifying system parameters in order to meet a library's unique needs. Non-turnkey systems need a considerable amount of local, onsite support, beginning with the installation of the system and continuing through the first year of operation. During this time, system bugs and the need for system modification will arise on a regular, almost constant, basis. Although some vendors offer on-site assistance and consultation for specific installation problems, the library will still need to invest a considerable amount of overall effort to implement the application software that will run the system.

In addition to the application software that will run the automated circulation system, the library's circumstances may require the purchase of additional software packages to support system functions. For instance, any library workstations that will be using modems to dial into the automated circulation system will require communications software. Workstations that are hard-wired into the computer system via telecommunications cables may require software that allows each workstation terminal to emulate a terminal or system supported by the larger computer system. If the library plans to provide library users with system-generated receipts for charged or discharged items, or use system-generated "hold" or "route" slips, it will need to purchase software that allows workstation printers to serve as "host" printers. This will provide printers with the capability to receive and print data directly from the system rather than being limited to simple screen prints from the workstation terminal. Although the communications and printer software packages will not require the same degree of effort to install or maintain as that required to install or maintain the automated circulation system software, the same tasks will need to be completed, including a detailed study of the software documentation, a thorough testing of the functions provided by the software, and incorporation of any software modifications that are necessary to support the library's unique needs.

VENDOR DOCUMENTATION

As soon as the project manager has been appointed officially to the leadership position for the implementation project, this individual's first task, in conjunction with developing an implementation plan and timeline, will be to learn as much as possible about the automated circulation system the library will be installing. There will be a definite urgency to beginning this learning process if the system the library has selected is not a turn-key system and must be modified to meet the library's unique needs. Although the systems staff and programmers will have the expertise to make the software adjustments that will be necessary to implement the system, the project manager will need to advise these experts as to precisely what library needs must be met by these modifications. One of the best ways for the project manager and any other project participants to acquire detailed information about the new automated circulation system is to explore, as thoroughly as possible, the vendor-supplied documentation that describes the applications software and explains how system functions will operate.

The preparation of vendor-supplied system documentation is usually the responsibility of the programmers instrumental to developing the application software. These individuals will have recorded detailed descriptive information about the software as the system developed, with the resulting documentation serving as both a developmental record and operational manual.[2] This may help to explain why vendor-supplied documentation is often incomprehensible to the novice user, "written as if the user already knew the system . . . inadequate, boring, poorly organized, poorly (if at all!) indexed, outdated, and often wrong."[3] Recently, there have been signs, as evidenced by the response of automated system vendors, that the multitude of user complaints over the years about vendor-supplied documentation have been heard and heeded. In the past few years, vendors have made substantial efforts to reformat and clarify their documentation, presenting the information in alternative ways that make sense to the purchasers of the systems and conveying the concepts in language that individuals without systems programming backgrounds will understand. Accurate, well-organized, illustrated, indexed, easy-to-understand vendor documentation is, thankfully, becoming more common. If, however, the documentation provided is not written in a way that will appear logical to library staff, or in a language that they can readily comprehend, re-packaging the information into a more relevant format will be part of the project manager and project team's responsibility during the implementation process. Poor or incomprehensible documentation will cause significant increases in the staff time and costs pertaining to implementation, maintenance, and use of the software supporting the system.[4] An initial investment of a few staff members' time to adapt or modify vendor-supplied documentation prior to the system's implementation will benefit the library by saving many hours of staff time that might have been spent wading through incomprehensible system documentation after the system has been implemented. The project manager and project team will also bear responsibility for developing documentation specific to the system's operation in their particular library, including detailed descriptions of policies and procedures that will support the operation of the new automated circulation system. This additional type of documentation will be discussed more thoroughly in Chapter 9.

The vendor should also have some mechanism in place for updating the documentation to reflect system changes, enhancements, and updated documentation to system customers. Once the updated information reaches the library, it is the library's responsibility to adapt or modify the updated information if necessary, and distribute it, as quickly as possible, to library units utilizing system documentation for the automated circulation system. This updating process will continue long beyond the initial implementation of the new system, and last throughout the duration of the library's use of the system. Documentation that is not current is not accurate, and is, for all practical purposes, worthless.

The information likely to be included in vendor-supplied documentation falls into the four basic categories that follow.[5]

1. System Specifications

Documentation detailing systems specifications will include information pertaining to: a) the hardware configuration necessary to support the system (including memory requirements, input/output peripherals, and storage media), b) the software and related programs needed to support the system (including assemblers, compilers, interpreters, and utility programs), and c) all input and data requirements.

2. Programming Information

Programming information will describe the purpose of the programs, and explain precisely how the system works by including all of the algorithms used to program system functions. This documentation should include: a) record layouts describing the arrangement of data in records (i.e., the length of each field and whether it requires alpha or numeric data), b) flow charts describing the processing flow, c) program source code listings detailing programming language instructions, and d) a program narrative that describes what the program does.

3. Test Documentation

Test documentation will include a description of the various tests the system has passed.

4. Operator's Instructions

Operator's instructions will provide complete information for: a) setting up the system hardware, b) loading and running each system program, c) processing each type of system transaction, d) backing up system data, and e) decoding error messages.

The project manager, members of the project team, and systems staff who will be helping install the application software should all have an up-to-date set of vendor-supplied documentation ready at hand. This documentation will be an invaluable tool to be referenced at every step of the implementation process.

TESTING/MODIFYING THE SOFTWARE

Before any steps are taken to install the new system in either the testing or production regions, library administration, in consultation with the project manager and systems staff, will need to make a decision about the scope of system implementation. If the new automated circulation system is one that offers various circulation functions as individual components or modules, for instance, a series of system functions grouped as basic circulation (charges, discharges, renewals, holds, etc.), course reserves, and bills and fines, will the library include all of the system modules in the initial installation, or will a phased approach be used? If a phase approach will be used, what timeline is considered optimal? When making these decisions, it is important to review the supporting system documentation in detail to determine if an option exists for module-by-module installation. In some systems, the modules are interdependent, and not bringing up one of the modules would require maintaining both online and manual systems—a labor-intensive option that may be impractical given limited staffing resources. For instance, it is usually difficult to separate the bill and fine function from the basic circulation functions. A separate manual file would be required to monitor charges, due dates, and overdues, thus defeating the purpose of implementing a system that claims as a major advantage the automatic monitoring of these activities. However, it may be possible to postpone the implementation of a relatively independent module such as course reserves. A simple method may be devised to record, within the automated circulation system, a "charge" to the reserve unit so that library users know the item has been placed in the reserve collection. Short-term loans within the reserve collection could continue to be recorded through whatever system, manual or computerized, the reserve unit currently uses. A decision about the implementation schedule for the individual system modules should be made as early in the implementation planning process as possible, as many of the tasks that follow, such as training, publicity, establishing policies and procedures, will depend largely on what functions will be activated at system start-up.

Once the scope of system implementation has been decided, and well before the system is used on a day-to-day basis, it is essential that the software be tested thoroughly, subjected to all the scenarios

```
FIGURE 4-1    Testing/Modifying the System


        SYSTEM FUNCTIONS                      SYSTEM TABLES

     Charge/Discharge                      Service Units
     "Browse"                              Location Codes
     Renewals                              Library Calendar
     Recalls                               Security-Individuals
     Holds                                 Security-Profiles
     Fines                                 Patron Categories
     Course Reserves                       Patron Blocks
     Item Records                          Patron Fines
     Patron Records                        Reports/Notices
     Overrides
     Flags/Action Dates




        PRINT PRODUCTS                       DISPLAY SCREENS

     "Courtesy" Notices                    Charge/Discharge
     Overdue Notices                       Recall/Hold
     Item Needed Notices                   Patron Records
     Item Available Notices                Item Records
     Bills                                 OPAC Messages
     Daily Operations Reports
     Statistical Reports




                        SYSTEM "FIXES"
```

that are likely to arise, both routine and exceptional, when the system is operational. This testing should include all functions within the application software that will be included in the initial or short-term implementation of the system. It will also be necessary to test all of the batch-processing programs that will be producing the system's print products (see Fig. 4-1).

TESTING THE APPLICATION SOFTWARE

The project manager, project team, and systems staff will need to work together closely, coordinating their activities when testing the application software of the new automated circulation system.

The systems staff will rely on project participants from the library to set up data files and scenarios that will be used to test the system. Library participants will rely on the systems experts to assist with the identification of any system deficiencies discovered during the testing, as well as the correction of any system errors revealed through this process.

A testing region should be created within the system where system functions can be tested and experiments conducted, and system modifications can be made and reversed without jeopardizing the integrity of the production or "real" databases that will be used for daily operations. Test files with both item and patron records that can be manipulated in every way conceivable will be needed in the testing region. The testing region and its databases may not be as large as the production region and its databases, however, the testing regions should mirror the production region in every other way for accurate test results. This includes scheduling any batch operations, such as index generation, that will be a normal part of activities within the production region. Although it may not be necessary to run the batch programs with the same frequency as would be normal in the production region, working with the systems experts to schedule such runs when needed to accurately portray the system's response to testing will be a necessary part of the testing process.

To test the system's application software, the project manager and project team should begin by listing all the functions the system can perform. This should be followed by the identification of scenarios in which these functions are likely to be used once the system is operational. To imitate these situations in a contrived manner, a "script" for testing system functions in these various scenarios should be developed. This script will be used in the testing process, providing the system operator with step-by-step data entry and sequenced system commands for each scenario. All possible exceptions to standard procedures should be included in the testing process in order to determine what effect different variations will have on any system function. Each system function should be tested thoroughly, under as many conditions as can be anticipated by the project manager and project team. Developing and using the testing scripts will be a joint effort of the project manager, project team, and systems/programming staff. After the data entry and system commands within the script have been entered into the automated circulation system, the effects each of these scenarios has on the system can then be observed and analyzed. This testing process serves a dual purpose. Project participants develop a keen awareness of how the system reacts to different situations *and* become more adept at troubleshooting system problems. In addition, system errors can be identified and corrected in a controlled setting prior to use of the system in daily operations.

Depending on the scope of system implementation the library will be undertaking, test scenarios should be devised for every conceivable situation within the ten general circulation functions that follow.

1. Charge/Discharge

This should also include any system function that allows for the recording of in-house use of materials, e.g., a "browse" function.

2. Renewals

Testing of the renewal function should include scenarios where renewals beyond the maximum number of renewals allowed per item (if applicable) are attempted.

3. Recalls

In addition to testing the placement of recalls on charged items, testing should also include functions that allow cancellation of recall requests or resequencing of recall queues (if allowed by the system).

4. Holds

Testing the placement of holds on library materials should include any functions that allow cancellation of hold requests or resequencing of hold queues.

5. Fines

The bill and fines functions should be tested for automatic creation or adjustment of bills and fines, as well as for any creation or adjustment of bills and fines as initiated by library staff.

6. Course Reserves

All functions for course reserves should be tested if the new automated circulation system includes a course reserves module and if that module is scheduled to be installed during the initial system implementation.

7. Item Records

Functions for creating and modifying item records should be tested.

8. Patron Records

Functions for creating and modifying patron records should be tested.

9. Overrides

Testing of override functions should include all overrides allowed by the new system, including those for charge/discharge date/time, patron blocks, renewal limits, and loan periods.

10. "Alert" Functions

Any system functions that allow library staff to enter "reminders" or "alerts" for themselves or other staff members should be tested. These "alerts" will include such things as action dates in item or patron records, flags for circulation or processing staff in item records, and active/expire dates in patron and item records.

TESTING THE PRINT PRODUCTS

Print products supplied by the system should be subjected to the same testing rigors as those employed for testing the system functions provided by the application software (see Fig. 4-2). In addition to ensuring that notices, reports, and other print products are actually produced without difficulty by the system, there is useful information to be gathered from thoroughly testing this aspect of the new automated circulation system.

First, by printing all the notices and reports provided by the system, the output can be reviewed and sorting orders determined. Are patron notices printed separately from the daily operations reports? Are the daily operations reports sorted by individual units? How are the patron notices sorted—by patron or by type of notice? Does the patron identification number or the alphabetical sequence of the patron's last name take precedence in the sorting? Are multiple items on a list of overdues sorted by call number, due date, or library location? If the system's default sort order is not in the library's best interests for efficient or cost-effective process-

---

FIGURE 4-2   Testing System-Supplied Print Products

PRINT PRODUCTS TO TEST

Notices
- —Overdue notices
- —"Courtesy" reminders
- —Item needed (recall) notices
- —Item available notices
- —Bills for fines, non-returned items, etc.

Daily Operations Report
- —System activity totals (charge, discharge, recall, hold)
- —System overrides and override totals
- —Bill and fine activity summary
- —Items discharged during charge process
- —Withdrawn items that were charged
- —Items that were charged to "lost" or "missing"
- —In-transit items not yet received
- —Items to be removed from hold shelf
- —Items with expired action dates

TESTS TO RUN

Notices
- —Are notices sorted by type of notice, service unit, patron name or identification number?
- —If there is more than one sort (sort orders within sort orders), in what order are the sorts sequenced?
- —Are items listed on notices sorted by owning unit, call number, barcode number?
- —What date is printed on bills, the transaction date or the date the bill was printed?
- —Are overdue notices printed for patron groups who do not accumulate fines?
- —Are "courtesy" notices printed at the correct time; e.g., three weeks before the due date?
- —Are special notes printed?
- —If there are multiple addresses recorded in a patron record, which address is printed on notices?
- —If there is an address override feature in patron records with multiple addresses, how does it work?
- —If a library user requests a missing book, does a notice print if the missing book returns and is discharged?
- —If temporary locations are used in item records, which prints on the notice, the permanent or temporary location?

Daily Operations Report
- —Are the reports sorted by service unit?
- —Do the system counts match actual activity; e.g., total number of charges, discharges, recalls, holds, etc.?
- —Is in-house use ("browse") reported as a separate category?
- —Do periods of very heavy activity impact the accuracy of the reported transactions?
- —Do the reported overrides match actual activity?
- —Are charges to "lost" and "missing" reported accurately?
- —Are "holds" that have expired reported?
- —Are items that are lost in transit reported?
- —If the system uses action dates, what happens when the action date expires?

ing and mailing, it may be possible to change it prior to system start-up. For instance, printing and mailing patron notices in zip code order may entitle the library to a discount, reducing postal charges.

In addition, testing is essential if the library prefers to add its own graphic touches to enhance the notices printed by the system. It is possible to program laser printers to work with the system software to produce polished, graphically-enhanced notices. If the library has this capability in-house or has the option through its parent agency, institution, or organization's computer center, it is worth pursuing. A polished, professional-looking notice commands respect and can improve the library's success in collecting fines or retrieving overdue items.

It is also necessary to test the circumstances under which notices are printed or not printed by the system. If there are situations in which the system prints notices that should not be mailed, staff can be trained to intercept such notices. For instance, if Patron B has had second thoughts about recalling an item from Patron A and has cancelled the recall after it has been entered into the system, how quickly must the cancellation be entered into the system to avoid generating a recall notice for Patron A? Knowing the system limits in such areas will avoid unduly harassing library users with obsolete notices.

Testing print products is also a good way to verify that the screen display accurately mirrors the system's response to a command. For instance, when a recall request is cancelled in the system by library staff and the display screen shows that the system has reverted to original due date (replacing the more immediate recall due date), has the system truly reverted to the original due date? In at least one commercially-available automated circulation system, the system will process overdue notices for the recall due date after the recall has been cancelled, contrary to the information (e.g., the reappearance of the original due date) that appears on the screen display. Staff in libraries using that particular software have learned to ignore the screen display and manually re-set the due date to avoid incorrect notices being generated.

TESTING SYSTEM "FIXES"

Most vendors, in response to system problems reported by customers, regularly provide system "fixes" that correct many of these problems. Whenever a system "fix," or any other system modifications or enhancements are to be installed, it is important that they be tested thoroughly and debugged in the testing region before they are installed in the production region. This considerably reduces the potential for unpleasant surprises ranging from minor inconvenience to major catastrophe when the new element is introduced in the production region. It has been wisely noted, "One site's fix is another site's bug."[6] In general, it's good policy to mandate that *every* system change, including changes to the application software, system tables, or display screens, be implemented and thoroughly tested in the training region prior to implementing it in the production region. This is an especially good policy to observe if the system program was written in assembly language. For these programs, the data must be "assembled" or compiled before a change is visible in the system. A routine change may take 24 hours or longer to finally appear in the system. Any problems, no matter how immediately obvious, will have to be suffered by staff until corrections can be processed. If the problem affects a basic function, such as charging materials, library staff and users will become frustrated by the system's "inefficiency." Scrupulous use of the testing region prior to implementing anything new in the production region will save many a headache.

SYSTEM TABLES

Not all automated circulation systems will depend on tables to run the software. Two examples that do, however, are the Dynix and NOTIS systems. Both are table-driven, allowing libraries to add a considerable amount of customization to the software products, unlike software packages where the parameters for patron groups, loan periods, and so on are coded into the programs.[7] With NOTIS, in particular, highly specific library circulation policies may be implemented within the system.

Typically, table-driven systems will include tables for the following types of data.

1. Library Units and Individual Workstations
Library units will need to be individually defined prior to entering this information into the system. A library unit can be defined as narrowly as a single workstation at a circulation service desk or as broadly as a group of workstations throughout a library building. When defining library units, one important factor to bear in mind is that the data provided by system-generated printed reports

will be grouped by the individual library units that have been defined in the tables. Whatever statistical breakdown is most meaningful for the library (by workstation, by service area, by library building) should be considered when defining library units for systems tables.

Individual workstations will also need to be identified for the systems tables. In addition to providing each workstation access to the automated circulation system, identifying individual workstations in systems tables will also allow security authorizations for specific circulation functions to be assigned to individual workstations.

If the automated circulation system is part of a larger integrated system, and its implementation follows that of other modules within the system, most of this data will already have been entered into system tables. All that need be entered into systems tables prior to implementing the circulation module will be a few additional pieces of data, such as specific circulation functions authorized for individual workstations.

2. Location Codes for Library Collections

Different circulation policies may apply to different types of materials within a library collection. These policies need to be identified by assigning location codes to different materials or areas within the collection. Location codes may be as general as a single location code for the entire collection within a building (such as "math" for all of the mathematics library materials) or as specific as individual materials within one collection (for instance, the circulating collection, desk reference collection, standards, dictionaries, directories, and so on within the sciences collection).

If the automated circulation system succeeds the implementation of other modules within an integrated system, this data will already be in place in the system tables. If the automated circulation system is the first module to be implemented as part of an integrated system, very careful consideration will need to be given to the future use of these location codes. Broad discussion among circulation, reference, and technical services staff should precede any decisions regarding the array of location codes that will be part of the automated circulation system.

3. Library Calendar

Data in the library calendar tables will detail the days and hours *each* library unit will be open. Any exceptions to routine hours, such as holiday closings, will also be included in the calendar tables. This data will be instrumental in calculating fines and due dates.

4. Staff Security Authorizations

Security tables will provide a means for assigning appropriate security profiles for each staff member who will have access to the automated circulation system. These profiles will authorize library staff to perform specific circulation functions. (See Figs. 4-3 and 4-4.) If the automated circulation system succeeds the implementation of other modules within an integrated system, this data will already be in place in the system tables. If the automated circulation system is the first module to be implemented as part of an integrated system, security authorizations specific to succeeding modules can be added to the tables as needed.

5. Patron Categories

Patron categories will be instrumental in determining loan periods, renewal limits, fines rates, and blocks to borrowing privileges. Patron categories should be assigned with meaningful differences in mind (e.g., the circulation policies or library services that will vary from group to group). In an academic library, for instance, circulation policies for students will probably differ from circulation policies for faculty. Conversely, in a public library, circulation policies and services for children may differ from circulation policies for adults. Sample patron groups for an academic library could include faculty, staff, graduate students, undergraduate students, and individuals not affiliated with the college or university but allowed borrowing privileges. Sample patron groups for a public library could include children under 12, children 12-17, adults 18-62, senior citizens, volunteers or friends of the library, companies, and individuals who live outside the library's home community.

Patron categories will include more than library users who ask to borrow materials. Patron categories will also be needed for staff groups or functions that will need to charge items through the automated circulation system. This will allow effective tracking of any library item, no matter why it is absent from the shelf. Sample patron groups in this area could include interlibrary loan, fee-based services, document delivery, bindery operations, and lost or missing materials.

Patron categories will also be used to generate some system reports. When defining patron categories for the system tables, keep in mind what categories would be useful for system-generated statistical reports.

(For more help determining patron categories, see the discussion of patron records in Chapter 6).

6. Patron Blocks

Data in these tables will detail parameters for blocking library users' borrowing privileges. This will include such factors as outstanding fines, maximum reached for number of items charged, expired patron records/identification cards, and so on.

7. Fines

The fines tables will include data concerning fines rates schedules, maximum and minimum fines, and any grace periods that may be allowed for the return of items past their due date.

8. Reports and Notices—Formatting and Frequency

The data in these tables will determine the formatting of system-generated reports and the frequency with which they are printed.

If the system the library has selected is table-driven, a significant amount of time will be spent gathering data for input into the tables. Much of the data collection process will lead to discussions concerning library policies and procedures. Depending on which group has been delegated the responsibility of recommending policies and procedures for use with the new automated circulation system, the project team or the circulation advisory group will need to review tables data for consistency within the library and for compliance with library policies. This process and the discussions that will be generated by it will also provide library staff with an opportunity to examine past practices and adapt or change them as necessary to meet new patron needs or system specifications.

Prior to beginning the data gathering process for tables construction, the following issues will require discussion and resolution:

1. definition of patron groups that will be used in the new system,
2. determination of loan codes and fines schedules for these patron groups,
3. location codes for specific library materials or collections, and
4. determination of loan codes and fines schedules as applied to location codes and/or individual libraries within large library systems.

Procedural decisions may also be necessary prior to entering data into the systems tables. For instance, decisions will need to be made concerning the frequency with which patron notices or lists of missing items are printed.

When constructing a multi-dimensional matrix that includes all the variables for determining an item's due date (patron group, item format, item location, owning library), one can quickly see the precision in complexity such an automated circulation system allows. This flexibility is an especially valuable feature for large library systems that consist of multiple libraries or collections and a variety of user groups. However, it also means that the tables in such a system must be monitored continuously to ensure that the data within them are accurate and reflect the library's current policies.

Tables data must be entered into the system prior to any use of the system functions. Even subjecting these data to testing prior to system start-up will not guarantee error- or problem-free tables. Changes are inevitable once the system is in daily use and the full impact of decisions made prior to the system's activation is realized. Changes are also dictated by any revision of library policies and procedures. For example, the public relations benefits thought to be realized by mailing three notices for each overdue item may diminish in importance after the system is in daily use and it is seen how this procedure seriously impacts a circulation unit's workload. It is a given that a certain portion of the decisions made prior to implementation will be changed once the system is activated in production.

SECURITY PARAMETERS AND PROFILES

System security will be a major concern when implementing a new automated circulation system. One facet of system security is the physical safety and securing of the system hardware discussed in Chapter 5. In addition to physically securing the system hardware, there is also the issue of securing the software and the item and patron databases from unauthorized tampering. This includes maintaining the privacy of information included in the patron database and ensuring that it is safe from unauthorized viewing. However, parallel to the need to employ security measures to prevent theft, tampering, or unauthorized access is the need to provide the best service possible to library users and to hamper library staff as little as possible in achieving this goal.[8]

Security of the system software and files can be achieved in two ways. The first form of security imposes controls via the system hardware (e.g., only specifically-designated workstations are allowed to perform certain system functions). To avoid use of these workstations by unauthorized individuals, terminals may be disabled or turned off and locked when they are not in use, especially after staff have left these areas for the day. The second method of security control involves authorizing each staff member to perform only those system functions necessary for their job duties. An individualized list of authorized activities for each staff member can be incorporated into the staff member's unique password, log-on, or system identification card. Most institutions employ a combination of workstation and staff authorizations.

To delegate specific system functions to individual workstations or staff members, authorization data must be entered into the automated circulation system. The project manager and project team will need to work with library managers to define exactly what the security authorizations will be for each workstation and each staff member. Workstations or staff members not needing access to circulation functions will also need to be included in this process. Most likely, it will be possible to group together staff with similar duties and workstations in similar service areas so that a few broad security profiles will cover the authorization needs of all staff members or workstations. For instance, reference staff and interlibrary loan staff will need different security authorizations to complete their daily tasks, but individual staff members who belong to one of these two groups will probably have the same authorization needs as other members within the same group. Defining authorization needs for circulation staff will be more complicated since it will be necessary to subdivide "circulation staff" into its various components for different levels of security authorization (e.g., student assistants, supervisory staff, unit managers, etc.).

Developing security profiles for groups of library staff is an imperfect science. Once the system is operational and judgements can be made about how well specific authorizations are functioning on a day-to-day basis, it will probably be necessary to fine-tune the original profiles. As a general rule of thumb when developing the initial security profiles, it is easier to start out restricting the degree and scope of security authorizations and loosen them once the system is in place and needs are defined by the unit's activities than it is to tighten up initially lax or looser security. For instance, caution is advised when initially assigning authorization to override certain system features. Once the system is operational and it is clear that student assistants at service desks are not being intimidated by loud or aggressive library users, the manager of the unit may decide that it is appropriate to authorize student assistants to override a library user's renewal limit under certain circumstances.

Who among the library staff will need access to the functions provided by the new automated circulation system? A list of units requiring access to the automated circulation system might include circulation and fines, course reserves, technical services, interlibrary loan, document delivery, and departmental libraries. Once these broad areas have been identified within a library or library system, each should be analyzed to determine whether or not one security profile is suitable for all staff working in that unit. Separate profiles will be needed for staff functioning at different levels of responsibility within an area (i.e., student assistants in processing areas, "front-line" staff at service desks, unit managers, etc.). Perhaps this is most easily determined by creating a comprehensive checklist of system functions and indicating whether or not an individual staff member needs access to each specific function (see Fig. 4-3). Once this has been recorded for each staff member and commonalities have been identified, group security profiles can be developed for those areas sharing similar responsibilities. Defining security profiles that are based on similar responsibilities rather than on individual units reduces the number of profiles needed. The fewer security profiles there are in an automated circulation system, the easier it is to monitor and update security data within the system. For instance, supervisors in interlibrary loan or document delivery service units may require the same security authorization, and, therefore, have the same profile as full-time circulation service desk staff. While analyzing individual profiles for commonalities, there may be some negotiating of specific authorizations needed in order to reduce the number of profiles. In addition, if certain features are tied together in the system (e.g., an authorization to override one function automatically carries with it the authority to override another function), trade-offs in service, security, and convenience need to be explored. It is critical that the appropriate level of security authorization be assigned for each staff member. If the library prefers to err on the strict side, authorizations cannot be so limited as to hamper routine tasks required of the staff member. Each staff member's security authorization should allow them to perform their usual tasks. Alternative procedures must be made available to staff unauthorized to perform certain system functions so that these staff members are able to provide efficient service when exceptional circumstances arise.

FIGURE 4-3   Defining Individual Security Authorizations

A checklist such as the one below (tailored to data included in NOTIS system patron records) can be used to determine exactly which patron record functions individual staff members will be able to perform. Note that authorization to enter data in some fields automatically includes authorization to enter data into other fields. Individual checklists can be batched when completed and examined for commonalities that will lead to broader security profiles.

NAME _____

1. Will this individual be authorized to CREATE patron records?

_____ No

_____ Yes

2. Will this individual be authorized to MODIFY patron records?

_____ No

_____ Yes

If the answer to either question #1 or #2 was "yes," continue with the following questions.

3. Into which patron record data fields will this individual be authorized to enter data (please check)?

_____ Name

_____ Social Security Number (SSN)

_____ Note

_____ Organization ID

_____ Department, Patr1, Patr2, Luis Message

_____ Patron ID, Category, ID Status

_____ ID begins, ID delete dates

_____ Address Information, Type, Mail, Address Dates

Even in a large, complex library system with many staff performing a wide variety of tasks, it is possible to distill most of the variations down to a few common profiles. For instance, the range provided by the six profiles in Figure 4-4 might cover all of a library's security authorization needs.

Once security profiles have been created and individual staff have been assigned appropriate profiles, staff will need instruction concerning: 1) the system's capabilities, 2) their individual security authorizations, and 3) alternative processes to use or individuals to contact if situation-specific access to a system function for which

---

FIGURE 4-4   Sample Security Authorization Profiles

PROFILE NAME: NONE

Staff are not authorized to perform any circulation functions. This category could include staff in reference, collection development, and library administration, as well as volunteers who will not be using the circulation system to perform their jobs.

PROFILE NAME: MINIMAL LEVEL I

Staff are authorized to: a) charge, discharge, renew, and recall/hold library materials; b) view and update selected fields in item and patron records; and, c) view bill and fine records. This category could include student assistants or volunteers in circulation, interlibrary loan, and document delivery library units.

PROFILE NAME: MINIMAL LEVEL II

Staff are authorized for all of the functions included in MINIMAL LEVEL I and, in addition, are authorized to: a) create item and patron records, b) update all fields in patron records, c) adjust patron bills, and, d) override blocked patron ID's, system date and time, due date calculation, and renewal limits. This category could include all non-supervisory staff in reserve, full-time staff and managers in interlibrary loan and document delivery, and full-time staff in circulation.

PROFILE NAME: MAXIMUM LEVEL

Staff are authorized for all the functions included in MINIMAL LEVEL II and, in addition, are authorized to: a) create patron bills, and b) perform all system overrides. This category could include managers in circulation, reserve, and staff in fines unit.

PROFILE NAME: PROCESSING

Staff are authorized for MINIMAL LEVEL I and, in addition, are authorized to: a) modify all fields in item records, and b) override due date calculations and renewal limits. This category could include all technical services staff who will be using circulation functions.

PROFILE NAME: ALL

Staff are authorized to perform all functions within the system. This category could include systems staff, the automated circulation project manager, and members of the project team. Individuals also may be granted this authorization on a short-term basis to meet the needs of a special assignment or project.

---

they are not authorized is needed. In addition, staff must be thoroughly indoctrinated on the importance of system security and must understand how important it is that their password, security card, or log-on be guarded and not shared indiscriminately. The most efficient security system will fail if staff liberally share their means of access.

REFERENCES

1. Compiled from Joseph R. Matthews, *Choosing an Automated System: A Planning Guide* (Chicago, IL: American Library Association, 1980): 88-89; and Carol Pitts Hawks, "Management Information Gleaned from Automated Library Systems," *Information Technology and Libraries* 7 (June 1988): 137.
2. Richard W. Boss and Judy McQueen, "Automated Circulation Control Systems," *Library Technology Reports* 18 (March/April 1982): 149.
3. Bonnie Juergens, "Staff Training Aspects of Circulation System Implementation," *Journal of Library Automation* 12 (September 1979): 206.
4. Boss, "Automated Circulation Control Systems," p. 149.
5. Compiled from Boss, "Automated Circulation Control Systems," p. 149; and Richard W. Boss, *The Library Manager's Guide to Automation,* Third Edition (Boston, MA: G.K. Hall & Co., 1990): 48-50.
6. Ellen Hoffman, "Managing Automation: A Process, Not a Project," *Library Hi Tech* 6 (1988): 48.
7. E. G. Fayen, "Automated Circulation Systems for Large Libraries," *Library Technology Reports* 22 (July/August 1986): 456.
8. Kathleen G. Fouty, "Online Patron Records and Privacy: Security vs. Service," *Journal of Academic Librarianship* 19 (November 1993): 289.

5 WORKING WITH THE SYSTEM HARDWARE

The system hardware for the new automated circulation system will consist of three major components:

1. the computer on which the system software will be installed and run,
2. the workstations that will be used to access the automated circulation system, and
3. the wiring that will connect the workstations to the main system computer.

Thoughtful planning should precede the selection and installation of these system hardware components, with skillful coordination of all the accompanying steps underlying the entire process. Responsibility for these tasks will fall to the systems office within the library, the project manager, or both.

MOUNTING THE SYSTEM SOFTWARE

Generally, decisions concerning what type of computer will be used to mount the system software and where that computer will be located will have been made prior to the implementation process. These issues are often resolved during the initial planning process when a specific automated system is selected for the library. Basically, two options exist. The library may choose to purchase, install, and maintain a minicomputer to run the new automated system, or contract with its parent agency, institution, or organization's computer center for the installation, and maintenance of the system software on a centrally-located mainframe computer. If the implementation of the new automated circulation system follows a series of previous automation projects, the circulation system software will probably be mounted in the same fashion as previously-installed software packages.

In 1986, the Association of Research Libraries found that among academic libraries there was an equal split between those who installed and maintained minicomputers within the library and those who contracted for the use of mainframe computers outside the library.[1] There are advantages and disadvantages to both scenarios. A minicomputer managed by the library offers a distinct advantage: the library is in total control of the computer system's time and capacity, and may use both as needed. No other users or projects compete for the computer's time or storage. However, the library is completely responsible for providing climate-controlled, secured space for the computer, any necessary electrical or telecommunications connections for the computer, whatever staff are required to operate and maintain the hardware and software for the system, and any supplies, equipment, or peripherals that are necessary to fully operate the system. Contracting time on a central computer center's mainframe computer means the library must compete with other users for computer system time and storage. However, it also offers the library a different advantage—the library is absolved of any responsibility for housing, maintaining, or operating the computer that will run the system. If the library has decided to contract time on a central computer center's mainframe computer, a formal memorandum of agreement between the library and the computer center, detailing what services will be delivered and when, will go a long way toward preventing serious time and storage problems (see Chapter 3 for a fuller discussion of this issue). In addition to drawing up a formal memorandum of agreement, immediately establishing a good working relationship between the library and computer center staffs will serve the library well when exceptional circumstances arise and special arrangements must be made.

HARDWARE FOR THE WORKSTATIONS

In conjunction with the process of deciding how and where the system software should be mounted, it is probable that a decision was also made concerning the hardware the library would purchase for staff workstations to access the automated circulation system. Although the details, such as specific models within a manufacturer's line, may change somewhat as lists of expected activities are identified for individual workstations, general guidelines should be available concerning what hardware will comprise a "typical" workstation and which vendors have been selected to supply the hardware. By the time the implementation stage is reached, the primary hardware decisions remaining will be the determination of the total number of staff workstations needed, the physical placement of each workstation, and the model numbers for the individual components within each staff workstation.

HOW MANY WORKSTATIONS DO WE NEED?

To determine the number of workstations that will be needed in each unit to support automated circulation activities, begin by assuming there is an unlimited source of funding for hardware purchases and identify the *optimal number* of workstations needed to support staff circulation activities as well as the *ideal* hardware configuration for each workstation. The vendor-supplied documentation for the new automated circulation system will assist the project manager and project team in determining workstation hardware requirements. Hardware specifications detailed in the system documentation should match those of the proposed components, including computer terminals, monitors, printers, scanners, and any other equipment that will be included as an integral part of a workstation. Bearing in mind the hardware requirements of the new automated circulation system, the number and type of workstations needed can be determined by asking the following questions:

1. Where will it be important for staff to have access to the automated circulation system? What areas will need workstations for providing circulation services to library users? What areas will need workstations for staff circulation activities?
2. What kind of traffic does each of the identified areas typically receive during the busiest time of day? Is overall use of individual workstations likely to be steady or sporadic?
3. What kinds of tasks will library staff be expected to perform at each workstation? Will these tasks consist of relatively simple routines (such as discharging library materials), or will tasks vary from simple to complex (for instance, a mix of straightforward charges, patron and item record creation, and fines negotiations)?
4. What is the maximum number of staff scheduled to work

in this area at any one time? How many of these individuals are likely to require simultaneous access to the automated circulation system? What number of workstations will be required to keep staff competition for system access and user queues to a minimum?

5. Are there likely to be "slow" times when this workstation could be used for activities other than circulation? Is a shared workstation a feasible option?

6. What type of hardware is likely to be required for providing back-up when the automated circulation system is down? Will "dumb" terminals suffice, or will the back-up program require a computer terminal?

7. What future system expansion or enhancements are likely? What type of hardware configuration will provide flexibility in meeting future system needs or requirements?

Now adopt an entirely different assumption, namely, that only extremely limited funding is available for hardware purchases, and determine the *minimal* number of workstations and *most basic* hardware configuration with which the library could function. Finally, with these two extremes in mind, aim for a middle ground that will achieve a realistic compromise between ideally-desired hardware purchases and probable budget limitations.

DEFINING MULTIPLE-PURPOSE WORKSTATIONS

Instead of designating one or more separate circulation workstations for each area within the library, it may be possible for a number of staff performing different functions at different times, including non-circulation functions, to share a common workstation. In smaller units, such as departmental libraries, it is relatively easy to perform all circulation tasks on only one or two workstations. The volume of activity at these smaller libraries is usually such that a common workstation can be used to charge and discharge materials, negotiate fines with patrons, process recalls and holds, and even answer general questions about the library collection if the automated circulation system also provides access to an online public catalog.

Sharing workstations is also possible in larger circulation units if some circulation functions, such as processing recalls and holds, are batched and processed during those times when staff competition for the workstation is considerably reduced. For instance, library staff could perform batched functions at terminals in service areas during early morning, late afternoon, or evening hours—

off hours when circulation transactions normally decrease. On the other hand, if a separate terminal is designated for discharging materials, this terminal could be used for other activities when materials are not being discharged.

Most circulation workstations will be subjected to both high-demand and slack times throughout the course of a day. By anticipating this ebb and flow, it is possible to schedule multiple circulation functions on a single workstation, thus saving the library the purchase price of an additional workstation that would not be fully utilized. The library will also be able to economize by eliminating the on-going cost associated with maintaining a workstation, as well as the electrical and telecommunications costs associated with activating a workstation.

PHYSICAL REQUIREMENTS FOR INSTALLING WORKSTATIONS

In addition to matching the workstation hardware to the system requirements, the physical dimensions of the hardware for each workstation should be matched to the space in which the workstation will reside. Make sure the physical space will accommodate all of the proposed components. This is particularly critical if the workstation will be placed on existing, built-in counter space and must fit within narrowly defined space limitations.

By previewing the final placement of the workstation, it is possible to eliminate problems before they occur. First, make sure there is space for all the hardware that will comprise the workstation. This may entail some creative rearranging, if possible, of the workspace in which the workstation will be housed. Room will be needed for all of the computer terminal components, including the monitor, CPU/disk drive, and keyboard. In addition, space must be made for the barcode scanner and whatever cabling device or box will connect it to the computer terminal. The physical space needed for the scanner may range from virtually nothing for a simple light pen, to a number of cubic feet to house a more substantial pedestal-type scanner under which materials are passed for barcode scanning.

If a printer will be attached to the computer terminal, space will need to be found for housing the printer and storing supplies such as paper, forms, and print ribbons or cartridges. A printer using continuous-feed paper or forms will need additional room to accommodate a ready supply of paper or forms. Workstations that serve library users, in particular those that provide the user with some sort of printed receipt, due date slip, or bill, will need access to a printer. Although there is no need to invest in expensive laser printers now that relatively low-cost, high-resolution dot matrix and ink-jet printers are available, it is important to bear in mind that whatever printer is selected should be capable of providing clear, legible print products for library users. This will eliminate the unpleasant confrontations that can result from illegible due date slips.

Once the space requirements for the workstation hardware have been defined, determine how many receptacles will be needed to provide electricity for powering the equipment. The number of receptacles and their location in relation to the placement of the hardware components and the length of the components' electrical cords must be determined. Consulting with an electrician will identify any special needs that may exist. Whether or not any of the workstation components will require their own circuits, or what the optimal placement might be for surge protectors are typical examples.

The next step is to determine how the workstation will communicate with the system. A telecommunications connection will be needed to connect the workstation directly to the system or to allow staff to use a modem to dial into the system if the workstation will not be directly connected. Depending on whether or not there is a printer attached to the workstation, and whether it or not it is to be a "host" printer, more than one telecommunication jack may be needed.

After the system requirements have been resolved, the environmental elements must be considered. Is there enough light in the area in which the workstation will be housed? Will sound baffles be needed to reduce printer noise in public areas? Is there adequate, convenient storage for supplies such as printer forms, paper, ribbons, print cartridges, barcodes, and so on? If anti-theft devices will be installed, their placement in the workstation space should also be considered.

HARDWARE REQUIREMENTS OF THE BACK-UP SYSTEM

There are numerous types of back-up systems available for libraries to use when, on occasion, the automated circulation system is not operational. (See Chapter 7 for a full discussion of back-up systems.) Personal computer-based systems are the most reliable and efficient of these. If the library decides to pursue this option for backing up the automated circulation system, the equipment purchased for individual workstations will need to take into account what hardware requirements are necessary to run the back-up system. At least one personal computer will be needed at each circulation service desk where the back-up system will be employed. This will ensure uninterrupted service to library users when the automated circulation system is down. Areas other than circulation service desks may be able to get by without utilizing the back-up program, especially if the downtimes are of short duration. Depending on the volume of activity at circulation service desks, a reduced number of service points may be offered during downtimes. Although a particular circulation service desk normally has three workstations available for charging materials, one may suffice during downtimes, reducing the need for personal computers at that service desk from three to one. Given an era of tight budgets and diminishing funds, larger libraries may not be able to purchase personal computers for the many workstations that will be needed. Carefully analyzing service needs that must be met during system downtimes may provide opportunities for creatively configuring workstations so that a mix of personal computers with the less costly "dumb" terminals will meet staff and user needs.

FUTURE EXPANSION OR ENHANCEMENT OF THE SYSTEM

If the library has chosen wisely, the automated circulation system purchased will allow for future expansion and enhancement as the library and its user needs evolve.

If the library is installing an online public catalog (OPAC) for the first time in addition to automating circulation functions, expect to experience dramatic increases in circulation activity as a result of the increased visibility of the collection. Even if the library already has installed an OPAC, it is not unusual for circulation transactions to increase once the circulation system is operational and library users have ready access to the circulation status of individual items.[2] As the number of circulation transactions increase, the system should be able to accommodate the installation of additional workstations to meet the increasing workload without system functions suffering or any significant degradation of system response time.

In addition to the system enhancement and expansion that occurs over time as needs change, the library may also adopt a phased approach to purchasing hardware for the new automated circulation system, thereby contriving a more scheduled system expansion. If the equipment budget for the new automated circulation system is very limited, hardware to support the automated circulation system may be purchased in stages. Initial purchases could include only what is absolutely necessary to meet the minimal, basic needs of the library and its users. Additional hardware purchases that allow the library to progress beyond this basic configuration could be made as funds become available.

ORDERING THE SYSTEM HARDWARE

The project manager, working in conjunction with whomever is ultimately responsible for processing the equipment order, will need to develop a schedule that encompasses everything from the initial equipment order to the final, full operation of all the hardware that will be needed to support the new automated circulation system. Allowing some flexibility for slipped deadlines, the schedule should include timelines for ordering, receiving, installing, and testing the equipment. The schedule will also need to take into account any peripheral or support work that needs to be completed prior to the installation of the equipment, such as electrical or telecommunications wiring. Once the schedule has been finalized, the project manager will assume responsibility for monitoring the process to ensure that all tasks are being completed as anticipated, and to adjust the schedule as necessary to accommodate any delays.

Determining specific hardware needs and processing equipment orders can not begin too early once system implementation is underway. Early ordering of the equipment that will support the new automated circulation system minimizes the negative impact of the inevitable delays. Models may be discontinued before orders are processed, orders may be delayed in library or vendor offices, or production and shipping of the equipment may take much longer than originally anticipated. Order system equipment early enough to ensure delivery well in advance of system start-up. This will allow adequate time for installation and testing of the equipment prior to staff training and system activation.

TESTING THE SYSTEM HARDWARE

Once the equipment arrives, it should be unpacked by previously designated individuals who will make sure all components have arrived safely. These individuals should compare the shipment against the original order and any accompanying invoices, thoroughly inspect all the components in the shipment and, when the equipment has been installed in the various workstations, thoroughly test the equipment to make sure everything is in working order.

STATIC ON THE SYSTEM

Two additional equipment-related concerns may arise after the hardware has been installed and the workstations are operational. Whether or not static electricity is going to present a problem will become evident after the equipment has been installed. This problem usually surfaces during cold, dry weather and is often worse in carpeted areas. In addition to being a shocking experience for the terminal operator, static electricity can also cause the equipment to perform in unexpected ways. To reduce or avoid this problem, some relatively simple solutions are available. Anti-static mats, especially helpful on carpeted surfaces, can be placed wherever the terminal operator sits or stands when using the terminal. Anti-static aerosol sprays are also available.

Another area that has proven problematic for many libraries, and one that is not as easily resolved, is interference between electronic security systems and computer terminals. This interference can cause security systems to malfunction. Fortunately, the reverse doesn't seem to be a problem (i.e., security systems don't cause automated circulation systems to malfunction). The problem seems to originate with personal computers rather than the less powerful "dumb" terminals, and appears to be linked to specific brands of personal computers. The interference becomes most evident when these personal computers are placed within ten feet of security gates. This can be a serious problem for libraries physically unable to provide the requisite ten feet of separation between system computer terminals and the security system. Most circulation desks have been positioned purposely, some as permanent building structures, within close proximity of security gates for convenient monitoring of individuals exiting the library.

If either incorporating additional space between the security system and the computer terminals or replacing personal computers with "dumb" terminals are not options, there are two other remedies that various libraries have tried with mixed success. Contact the vendor of the security system and ask to have a technician adjust the antennae inside the security system's posts. The antennae are positioned to pick up signals from targeted library items within a certain range (for instance, anywhere within a range of one to five feet from the floor). Reducing the parameters of the sensitized field may help, the tradeoff being that it will also narrow the range in which targeted library items are detected. It is possible that the antennae may be adjusted in such a way as to eliminate system interference without sacrificing much of the detection field.

Another possible remedy that may prove successful on its own, or in conjunction with the adjustment of the security system antennae, is to build or purchase a three-sided, aluminum-lined box that will enclose the top, back and both sides of the computer terminal. The aluminum will intercept or block the signals given off by the computer terminal, reducing or eliminating system interference.

Unfortunately, there is no one solution to this problem. Different techniques may be needed in different libraries, or even for different workstations within a single library. Experiment to find the optimal solution for a particular situation.

WIRING

To operate the system equipment and access the automated circulation system, the necessary electrical wiring and telecommunications connections must be in place. If the new automated circulation system is a second or third generation automated circulation system, or if its implementation follows that of other modules within an integrated system, most or all of the telecommunications or electrical work has probably been completed. If not, the system requirements identified at the beginning of the equipment ordering process need to be reviewed and wiring work orders placed. Even if it's likely that all of the required wiring has been done earlier, a thorough examination should be conducted of all the areas in which equipment for the automated circulation system will be placed. Checking now to ensure adequate electrical and telecommunications outlets are available to support the automated circulation equipment will eliminate the possibility of unpleasant surprises at the last minute.

TELECOMMUNICATIONS WIRING

Connecting workstations to the computer running the automated circulation system software can be accomplished by a direct cable connection (the most reliable method), a private or leased telephone line where a modem provides the connection to the system, or a local area network (LAN).[2]

If the library decides to use a direct cable connection, or hard-wire library terminals to the main computer, cable will have to be strung throughout the library. This can be quite a job, both time-consuming and messy, as the cable's route will take it along and through walls, ceilings, and floors. Older buildings, with their unique architecture and possible lack of up-to-date duct work or schematics, present even greater wiring challenges.

If the library is part of an agency, institution, or organization that requires such jobs to be bid for by contractors, the process of soliciting and evaluating bids will add additional time to the task of telecommunications wiring. Also, wiring for telecommunications may involve both electricians and telecommunications technicians, making the wiring process a multi-part task. Scheduling the tasks in the appropriate sequential order may involve extended waiting periods between jobs, depending on the project backlogs of the involved workers. Work orders or bids for telecommunications wiring should begin as soon as the wiring requirements have been identified.

ELECTRICAL WIRING

Naturally, the library will have some electrical wiring in place prior to implementing the automated circulation system. The important task here will be to make sure there are enough receptacles to handle all the pieces of equipment that require outlets and that they match the electrical requirements of the system. Surge protection has become an accepted practice for computer equipment, no matter how reliable the source of electricity. However, the library will want to take special precautions if power fluctuations or surges are routine events. Surge protectors, either simple strips of outlets plugged into a receptacle, or the those wired directly into wall receptacles, will need to be ordered and installed.

If electrical failures or brownouts are a regular occurrence and will cause serious disruption of circulation activities, the library may want to consider installing a transformer, voltage regulator, or emergency generator.[3]

Electricians are usually in demand, so it is advisable to place work orders as soon as wiring requirements have been identified.

SECURING THE SYSTEM HARDWARE

Once the wiring has been completed and the equipment has been installed and tested, measures should be taken to ensure that the equipment is secure, safe from theft, and tampering.

If possible, the workstations should be placed in areas where they are under constant staff surveillance. Access to staff workstations in public areas should be restricted by whatever means are available. If a gate or door leads into the workstation area, make sure it is closed, and, during hours of low activity, locked. If there is no reliable way to secure the workstation area or if doing so would inhibit user access to the library or its services, there are numerous devices on the market that securely attach computer terminals to work surfaces, lock disk drives, and disable keyboards. Discouraging unauthorized use of a staff terminal can be as simple as removing the keyboard when the terminal is not in use and locking it in a drawer or cabinet. Determining who is and isn't an authorized member of the circulation staff may not prove as easy in larger circulation units where there are many staff members. This may become complicated in libraries where large numbers of student assistants are employed as short-term staff. All staff, including student assistants, should be trained to politely question anyone they do not recognize in a staff area.

If equipment theft is a concern, discourage would-be thieves by installing only the library's most humble equipment in public areas. Large, unattractive terminals discourage theft, as do older models, and "dumb" terminals. When this strategy is not possible, the library may want to invest in devices that physically bar the removal of equipment, such as a lock-down devices. As an added precaution, target strips normally placed in library items can be placed inconspicuously on each separate component of the computer terminal or its peripheral equipment.[4] Any unauthorized attempt to remove targeted equipment components will set off security system alarms, alerting library staff to the attempted theft.

When keys are part of the equipment security program, it is important that they not be left in easily accessible or obvious locations. In addition, they are best left unlabelled, or labelled with codes that only library staff understand.

SYSTEM SUPPLIES AND FORMS

The hardware components selected to support the new automated circulation system will be unable to function without adequate supplies and forms to support their functions.

SUPPLIES AND ADDITIONAL EQUIPMENT

Supplies that will be necessary for the operation of the system in circulation units include any paper or special forms that will be necessary for the printers, ribbons, or print cartridges for the printers, card stock for library-issued borrowers cards, and a multitude of barcode labels to affix to library items and library borrowing cards.

Consider purchasing one or more folder/stuffers to prepare notices for mailing if the library will not be using print-through mailers. By designating one unit as the recipient of all the circulation print products, staff time and energy can be saved, and print products distributed more efficiently. The central receiving unit could separate the daily operations reports by individual units and distribute them accordingly. The central receiving unit could also save staff time by sending patron notices directly from the unit, without distributing them to the "owning" units for mailing. In a situation such as this, a machine that folds and stuffs notices could prove to be a worthwhile investment.

FORMS

Two types of forms will be needed for circulation activities in the new automated environment. Forms that will be used to enter circulation information into the system will need to be designed and printed, and forms that will be used to print notices, bills and system reports will need to be designed and entered into the system.

Forms that will be used to collect circulation information prior to its entry into the automated circulation system will include forms for entering patron records, or for processing recall or renewal requests. Some of these forms, such as the form for collecting information for patron records, will not have been used before and must be newly-created. Forms that are already in use to collect circulation information, for instance, recall or renewal forms, will need to be reviewed in light of the new system. If this is the library's first automated circulation system, forms will have to be revised to include patron and item barcode numbers where appropriate (see Figs. 5-1 and 5-2). In addition, some information (for instance, individuals' addresses on renewal forms) may be eliminated once the system is activated and that information is included in system records. Since new forms require time to design and print, the development of new forms should begin at least three months prior to the system's activation. The widespread availability of desktop publishing software and laser or laser-quality printers make this an easy, relatively inexpensive task for most libraries.

After currently-used forms are reviewed with respect to the automated circulation system, thought should be given to additional forms that will be necessary for the system-supplied print products, such as due date receipts, item needed and item available notices, courtesy and overdue notices, and bills. Unless major policy or procedure revisions are anticipated, order enough of the new forms to last all units for the first year the system is in operation. A few months prior to the depletion of the forms, the same evaluation process should be undertaken, any revisions or additions made, and more forms printed.

REFERENCES

1. Association of Research Libraries, Systems and Procedures Exchange Center, *Automated Library Systems in ARL Libraries,* SPEC Kit #126 (Washington, D.C.: Association of Research Libraries, Office of Management Studies, Systems and Procedures Exchange Center, July-August 1986): 1-2.
2. John Corbin, *Implementing the Automated Library System* (Phoenix, AZ: Oryx Press, 1988): 83-4.
3. John Corbin, *Developing Computer-Based Library Systems* (Phoenix, AZ: Oryx Press, 1981): 92-3.
4. Corbin, *Implementing the Automated Library System,* p. 105.

FIGURE 5-1 Sample Renewal Form

UNIVERSITY OF MINNESOTA LIBRARIES

RENEWAL REQUEST

Renewal Limits
Books can be renewed only two times after initial check out. Attempts to renew books more than twice will result in overdue fines.

Renewal Due Date
Check at the Circulation Desk for new date due. Patrons are responsible for knowing the new due date.

Change of Address
If you have moved, a University change-of-address form can be filled out at Circulation.

PATRON NAME: _____
                         (Last)   (First)   (M.I.)

> PATRON
> BARCODE #: _ _ _ / _ _ _ _ / _ _ / _ _ _ _ / _ _

ITEM
BARCODE #: _ / _ _ _ _ / _ _ _ / _ _ _ / _ _ _ / _
    Author: _____
    Title: _____

ITEM
BARCODE #: _ / _ _ _ _ / _ _ _ / _ _ _ / _ _ _ / _
    Author: _____
    Title: _____

ITEM
BARCODE #: _ / _ _ _ _ / _ _ _ / _ _ _ / _ _ _ / _
    Author: _____
    Title: _____

ITEM
BARCODE #: _ / _ _ _ _ / _ _ _ / _ _ _ / _ _ _ / _
    Author: _____
    Title: _____

ITEM
BARCODE #: _ / _ _ _ _ / _ _ _ / _ _ _ / _ _ _ / _
    Author: _____
    Title: _____

ADDITIONAL SPACES FOR RENEWALS ON BACK

FIGURE 5-2   Sample Recall Form

UNIVERSITY OF MINNESOTA LIBRARIES
RECALL / HOLD REQUEST

PATRON
BARCODE #   — — — / — — — — / — — / — — — — / — —

NAME: _____

ADDRESS: _____

_____

LOCATION: _____

CALL NUMBER: _____

_____

AUTHOR: _____

TITLE: _____

I would like this item to be placed on:

_____ Recall   _____ Hold

If other copies become available, I want them from:

_____ this library only.

_____ any University of Minnesota—Twin Cities library
(NOTE: Recalls on copies at other locations must
be picked up at the owning library).

Date after which item is not needed: _____

OFFICE USE

A recall could not be placed:

_____ item is not currently checked out. Please contact Circulation
at_____ to place a search.

_____ missing information. Please verify and resubmit.

_____ blocked library privileges. Please contact Circulation
at_____

_____ OTHER _____

6 WORKING WITH THE LIBRARY'S RECORDS

Conversion of a library's files to machine-readable form is frequently the single most difficult problem in implementing a new circulation system. Depending on the size of those files, it may also be the most expensive.[1]

MACHINE-READABLE DATABASES AND FILES

A variety of data must be entered into the new automated circulation system before the system is capable of performing circulation functions or providing complete, accurate circulation information. Two fundamental data files—the item record database and the patron record database—will form the basis from which the new automated circulation system will operate. Reduced to its most basic level, the automated circulation system will repeatedly link and unlink records in these two databases as library materials are charged and discharged. All attendant system functions (i.e., recalls, holds, renewals, overdues, and billing) will be based on these linkages. Preparing for the implementation of the new automated circulation system will include converting the library's bibliographic records into a machine-readable format. In addition, it will be necessary to create a file of patron records detailing important information about individual library users and their borrowing privileges. As part of the process of creating electronic bibliographic and patron records, the library will also have to assign a unique identification number to each record within the bibliographic and patron databases. This is accomplished by placing a machine-readable identification label, either an optical character recognition (OCR) or barcode label, on each library item or library user identification card. The number on the identification label will then be entered into the corresponding database record for the item. If the library has implemented other modules of an integrated system prior to implementing the circulation module, or if the new automated circulation system will be a second or third generation system, some or all of these electronic records may already be available and the attendant barcoding completed.

In addition to the item and patron record databases that will form the backbone of the system and allow new transactions to be recorded online, other existing files will need to be converted to machine-readable format. Files created with the existing circulation system will include current information about charged and overdue materials, holds, recalls, outstanding fines and bills, and (if the library is part of an educational institution) materials on course reserve. Entering this information into the new automated circulation system will ensure the provision of accurate, up-to-date circulation information by the new system.

DATA REQUIREMENTS IN THE NEW SYSTEM

Prior to initiating a project to enter machine-readable bibliographic or patron records into the new automated system, the project manager will need to determine two things: what type of data will be necessary for system operations and what type of data will be required by the library for operational or statistical purposes. Close examination of these two areas will assist in defining exactly what data elements are essential for inclusion in machine-readable bibliographic and patron records. The system requirements will be fairly straightforward, and should be evident from the documentation provided by the system vendor. Determining the library's data requirements will require more thought. When analyzing the data needs of the library, be sure to include all data that will allow the system to generate informative notices for library users, any data that will enable the system to provide useful statistical summaries and reports for library managers, and all data that is routinely reported to agencies external to the library. When feasible or predictable, also include any anticipated future data demands, such as the implementation of additional system modules or system upgrades. Including these data elements in system records now will reduce or eliminate the need for another similar project at a later date.

Once the level of detail has been defined for the bibliographic and patron records that will be used by the automated circulation system, the format in which existing records are available will need to be reviewed and a conversion process selected. Are current records available in any type of machine-readable format, however limited, either within the library or from another source, or are only print records available? The current format of existing records will help determine the selection of the most appropriate conversion method.

PREPARING TO CONVERT OR CREATE SYSTEM RECORDS

It is critical that much thought and planning undergird whatever method is selected for the conversion process, since "there are no panaceas, no cheap shortcuts, and no ways to finesse the problem."[2] The bibliographic record conversion project will be, potentially, one of the most complex and demanding tasks required prior to implementing the new automated circulation system. At the outset of any project to create or convert records that will be used by the new automated circulation system, study the literature, talk to other librarians, and visit other libraries where similar projects have been undertaken. This will help determine what strategy is most appropriate for the situation in your own library. Ask for copies of procedures and manuals used in other libraries' conversion projects, and ask the staff in these libraries what errors are possible and how they can be avoided.[3] After analyzing the information gathered and molding it into a procedure for your own library, make sure staff who will be participating in the project are thoroughly trained in the procedures that have been developed and understand completely the importance of accuracy when completing their assigned tasks. In addition, supervision of project workers and periodic spot-checks of system records is a must to ensure that individuals participating in the project have fully comprehended their instructions and are matched to tasks for which they are most suited. A procedure manual, with clear, well-written instructions, will supplement training and direct supervision of project participants, providing answers to questions as they arise.

RETROSPECTIVE CONVERSION OF BIBLIOGRAPHIC RECORDS

If, as part of an integrated system, the library has already implemented automated systems for other library functions (for instance, cataloging, acquisitions, serials check-in, or the public catalog), the library may have many or all of its bibliographic records in machine-readable format. Machine-readable records also may exist if the new automated circulation system is a second or third generation system. Even if the new automated circulation system is the first step toward automating many library functions, it is possible that machine-readable bibliographic records exist as a result of a conversion project that anticipated these future automation projects. Any machine-readable bibliographic records created prior to the implementation of the new automated circulation system will need to be reviewed in light of the data requirements of this new system. It is possible that the new system will require information in addition to that already included in these records. Whether newly-created, or already in existence, machine-readable bibliographic records should be detailed to the item record level. Item records define individual volumes within a bibliographic record and are necessary for the functioning of automated circulation systems (i.e., they allow the system to circulate and maintain records on individual volumes within the library collection).

If the library is undertaking its first retrospective conversion project in conjunction with the implementation of the new automated circulation system, a good deal of thought will need to be devoted toward the construction of the bibliographic records and the accompanying item records. In addition to structuring these records with their immediate use in mind, consideration of the potential future uses of these records may minimize the chances of having to modify or re-construct the records when additional library functions are automated. As more libraries move towards integrated systems that require fuller records than the brief records traditionally used by stand-alone circulation systems, potential future uses of bibliographic and item records is an important factor to consider if automation of circulation activities is the first of many automation projects.

METHODOLOGIES FOR RETROSPECTIVE CONVERSION OF BIBLIOGRAPHIC RECORDS

Selecting an appropriate methodology for retrospectively converting bibliographic records depends on the answers that can be given to five questions.

1. What does the library own?

How many items comprise the total collection of the library? How many of those items are likely to require machine-readable records in the database (i.e., which items will it be desirable to track through the new automated circulation system)?

2. What is the current format of records for individual items within the library collection?

Are the current records in machine-readable format? If not, can machine-readable records be obtained from another source, such as a commercial vendor?

3. How accurate are the current records?

Have records been kept up-to-date? How recently were the records used to inventory the collection?

4. How complete are the current records?

Are these records from the catalog or the shelflist? Do they contain the level of detail that is required of records that will be entered into the new system?

5. What is the optimal number of records that should be in the database by system start-up?

What is the volume of circulation activity in the library? Will creating bibliographic records as needed to circulate individual items generate long queues at service desks? How much control is desired over the quality of the records in the database? Conflicting ideas exist as to just how much of a library's collection should be represented by records in the database before the system is activated. Studies show that circulating items in an academic library account for a small portion of the available collection, perhaps as little as one-fifth of the collection.[4] Depending on how much time the library wants its staff to spend creating records "on the fly" (i.e., as they are needed to circulate individual items), a reasonable target would be to convert approximately 50 percent of the collection records to machine-readable format prior to the implementation of the new automated circulation system.[5] If it will not be possible to have every record in the database at system start-up, it would be useful to approach the conversion project systematically, for instance, by converting all records from a specific publication date forward.

Depending on the answers to these five questions, there are three basic approaches to choose from when undertaking retrospective conversion of bibliographic records:

1. Create complete bibliographic records for all items included in the library collection (i.e., a comprehensive retrospective conversion of library records).
2. Create complete bibliographic records for a portion of the library collection (i.e., a partial retrospective conversion of library records).
3. Create brief, truncated records for the entire library collection (i.e., an abbreviated retrospective conversion of library records).[6]

The process of actually converting the library records to a machine-readable format can be accomplished by using one of the four approaches that follow.[7]

1. The As-Needed Approach

Records can be converted "on the fly" (e.g., as they are needed) in circulation units and at circulation service desks. This approach is a time-consuming process that can generate long queues at busy service desks. It also requires that all service desk staff be either: a) trained and authorized to create some form of bibliographic record, or b) provided with an alternative method for recording the data about the item and its circulation.

2. The Matched Record Approach

Machine-readable databases supplied by commercial vendors can be loaded and "matched" to locally-owned records. This approach can temporarily decrease response time for the system into which it is being loaded. It will also increase the labor costs of the conversion process since staff will be needed on-site to undertake the matching process.

3. The Commercial Firm Approach

This approach consists of relinquishing the entire conversion process to a commercial firm specializing in data conversion. Currently-existing collection records, such as a shelf-list or an existing machine-readable file, are sent to the company selected to undertake this project. They then convert the records to whatever format is specified. Contracting the conversion project to an outside firm is the quickest, most convenient approach to retrospective conversion, but it allows library staff very little control over the conversion project. Contracting the services of an outside firm may appear to be more expensive than mounting an in-house conversion project. However, the "hidden" costs of an in-house conversion project can mount as work backlogs build once library staff and equipment are removed from their primary units and dedicated to the retrospective conversion project.[8]

4. The Combination Approach

It is not unusual for a retrospective conversion project to embody elements from two or three of the previous approaches. For instance, the conversion of a portion of the total library records may be combined with the creation of the rest of the records by library staff on an as-needed basis. This is a reasonable approach for smaller libraries, and can even be used in larger libraries if the major portion of the circulating collection is converted before the system is implemented. Most libraries will create some records on an as-needed basis—no matter how thorough a retrospective conversion project has been undertaken. Temporary, or even permanent records, may be needed as policy exceptions are made for items that ordinarily do not circulate, and which may not have item records in the database. Reference materials, items in micro or electronic format, or unbound issues of periodicals may be included in this category. If it is desirable to track these loans through the automated system, staff may need to create a record as each item circulates. Circulation and technical services staff will need to consult with each other and decide just how extensive a record is required. Will a temporary item record with limited use and access and without a link to a bibliographic record suffice, or must a fuller, more permanent bibliographic record be created, with individual item records linked to the bibliographic record? Turf battles and concerns for the integrity of the bibliographic database can be avoided if this decision and the resulting procedures are discussed and agreed on by all affected parties in circulation and technical services.

Unbound issues of periodicals pose their own problems. Unless the library has a relatively small, manageable periodical collection, it will be a cumbersome task to create machine-readable records for each issue within a single title prior to the implementation of the automated circulation system. These records could clutter the database in a larger collection if the library regularly binds individual issues. In addition to creating many records that may never be used, some mechanism will be necessary for the withdrawal of these individual records after they are bound into a single volume. In larger collections, it may be more feasible to create temporary, unlinked item records as individual unbound issues circulate. Depending on how the collection is used and the politics governing their use, these difficulties may be avoidable entirely by prohibiting circulation of any unbound issues of periodicals.

After the records have been converted, it is important to check and verify the converted records to ensure that they are complete and free of errors.[9] This verification process is particularly important for those records that have been converted to machine-readable format by a commercial firm. Any errors or incomplete records, no matter how they were converted, should be identified and corrected at the first opportunity.

BARCODING THE COLLECTION

This section will provide an overview of barcodes and the barcoding process, rather than a comprehensive explanation of how to barcode the library's collection. Excellent, in-depth discussions of the barcoding process are available elsewhere in the library literature. The bibliography at the conclusion of this book includes a selective sampling of some of these publications. The process of barcoding a library's collection will require physically handling each volume in the collection and will involve: 1) matching the volume to a corresponding item record in the system (or creating a record if none exists), 2) placing a scannable, machine-readable label on the volume, and 3) entering the unique identification number printed on the label into the online item record. When planning the barcoding project, bear in mind that this particular phase in the implementation project is often the most visible portion of the system implementation for library users. Careful planning can result in a project that portrays the system in a positive light, and, ultimately, assists in promoting early acceptance of the system by both library users and staff.[10]

The majority of libraries select barcodes rather than OCR (optical character recognition) labels even though most automated systems are designed to read either barcodes or OCR labels. Even though the information included in OCR labels is easily read by the naked eye, OCR technology costs more, requires more complicated equipment to scan the label, and carries a high rate of scanning error since the imprints are difficult to scan accurately.[11] Barcodes only allow for a limited amount of information to be encoded in the series of stripes that comprise the barcode (typically 18 characters). The fact that the information must be coded means it cannot be read by the naked eye, but must be scanned into the automated system. However, barcode technology is much less expensive than OCR technology, and the imprints are much easier to scan, resulting in a minimal error rate. As a result of their relatively low cost, and their suitability for libraries of all sizes, barcodes are used almost universally to identify individual library items.[12]

"Smart" Versus "Dumb" Barcodes

The major decision for those barcoding their collections is whether "smart" barcodes or "dumb" barcodes will be used (see Fig. 6-1). "Smart" barcodes are those that have been printed to match specific volumes in the collection. The string of identification characters on each barcode label will have been entered into a specific item record in the database prior to the application of that barcode label on the physical piece. Before the smart barcode can be applied to the physical piece, the record in the database and the volume on the shelf will need to be matched. A "dumb" barcode, on the other hand, can be applied to any physical item in the collection since the string of identification characters printed on the barcode label is entered into the item record *after* the barcode label has been applied to the physical piece. The dumb barcode label serves as a "tabula rasa" on which the information about any item within the collection can be encoded. The link between an item record in the database and the physical item on the shelf is established after the barcode has been applied to the physical item.

There are advantages and disadvantages to both types of barcodes, and neither approach is foolproof. Smart barcodes may be perceived as labor intensive to apply since they require an initial outlay of staff time for the matching process. However, the matching process mandated by the use of smart barcodes allows the library to conduct an inventory of the collection, yielding a much cleaner database by the time the project is finished. Dumb barcodes on the other hand, initially are much easier to apply. However, staff effort still must be expended at the other end of the project to link a record within the database to a physical item

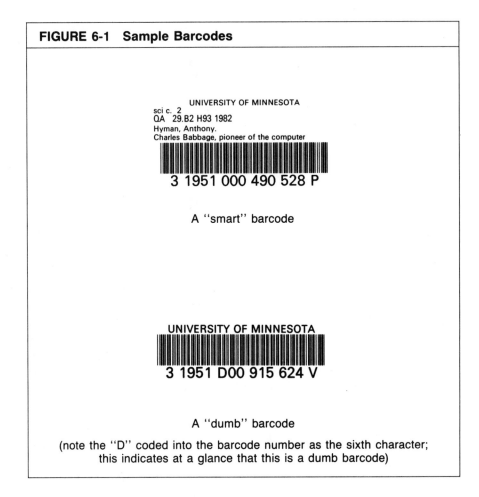

FIGURE 6-1   Sample Barcodes

UNIVERSITY OF MINNESOTA
sci c. 2
QA 29.B2 H93 1982
Hyman, Anthony.
Charles Babbage, pioneer of the computer

3 1951 000 490 528 P

A "smart" barcode

UNIVERSITY OF MINNESOTA

3 1951 D00 915 624 V

A "dumb" barcode

(note the "D" coded into the barcode number as the sixth character;
this indicates at a glance that this is a dumb barcode)

within the collection. After applying a dumb barcode, a corresponding record for the physical piece must be located or created in the automated system and the string of identification characters on the barcode label entered into that record.

If smart barcodes will be utilized, a process for printing these labels must be identified. To print barcode labels that match specific items within the collection, it will be necessary to submit a machine-readable database to the vendor selected to print the barcode labels. The database will need to include individual item records containing all the information that will be encoded in the barcode label. If most or all of the collection records will be in machine-readable format prior to beginning the barcoding project, smart barcodes will be the most efficient, accurate way to barcode the collection—assuming that the database from which the barcodes are printed is accurate and up-to-date.

PLACEMENT OF THE BARCODE ON THE PHYSICAL PIECE

Deciding where to locate the barcode label on the physical item is bound to generate lively discussion among library staff members. A careful, step-by-step analysis of the library's charging and discharging procedures should precede any decision on barcode placement. Most libraries place their barcodes on the inside of the front or back cover, arguing that this both protects the barcode from damage and is conveniently located near the placement of the date due slip.[13] However, if the removal of date due slips from book pockets will not be a routine part of the library's discharge procedure, it will add an unnecessary step to the charging/discharging process if staff are required to open the front or back cover of every item in order to scan the barcode. It may be better to place the barcode on the outside of the item, for example, at the top center of the back cover, to allow for quick and easy scanning of large groups of items. If an externally-applied barcode does sustain damage, replacing it is relatively easy and inexpensive. Since a record for the item already exists in the automated system, all that needs to be done is to replace the damaged barcode number with the replacement barcode number. Some automated circulation systems automatically transfer any circulation information entered under the previous barcode to the new barcode so that none of the circulation history for that item is lost when the barcode is replaced. In an effort to extend the life of barcode labels placed on outside covers, however, additional protection can be applied. Some libraries have experimented successfully with the placement of clear plastic tape over the barcode. The tape protects the barcode, yet allows unimpeded scanning.[14]

PLANNING THE BARCODING PROJECT

Many of the following questions need to be answered prior to planning a barcoding project:

1. Will the project be a long-term effort, spread out over many months or years, or will it be a short-term, intensive effort, concentrated within in a few weeks or months?
2. If the barcoding project is to be a long-term effort, will barcoding tasks be incorporated into existing staff responsibilities?
3. If the barcoding task is to be a short-term effort, will staff be reallocated to the project from other areas of the library, or will "volunteers" be recruited to donate their time during hours they would ordinarily not be scheduled to work?

4. If using existing staff is not feasible, will a special, temporary team be hired to handle the barcoding process, or will volunteers be recruited from the community, or parent institution or organization?
5. Will the library remain open for business as usual, or will doing so increase the potential for serious disruption of library services?
6. If the library is to remain open, either fully or in a limited capacity, what special services will be required to minimize the disorder that will inevitably accompany the project (for example, on-demand paging of items that have be moved to restricted areas as part of the project)?
7. If neither has been undertaken within the past year or two, will it be feasible to conduct a complete inventory or shelf-read the entire collection prior to applying the barcode labels?

If the library budget and implementation project timeline allows for it, conducting a complete inventory or shelf-reading the collection prior to applying the barcode labels will set the stage for a quicker and more efficient process for applying barcode labels. The smart barcoding process will virtually mandate an inventory of the collection, whether it is conducted as a separate project preceding the application of the barcode labels, or is undertaken concurrent with the application of the barcode labels. In either case, a pilot project testing the barcode label application process in a single collection within the library or in a branch library within the library system, will help identify potential problems that may arise during the full-scale application process. A pilot project will also assist in finalizing the procedures that will be used to complete the larger project.

Likely problems in any barcoding project, whether short-term or long-term, center on human or system errors. A sample of barcoding problems might include barcodes that have been printed incorrectly (especially problematic if smart barcodes are being applied), physical pieces that are missing or misshelved, information that has been incorrectly entered into the system record for an item (either the description of the item or the barcode number), and barcodes that have been applied to the incorrect physical piece. The more long-term the barcoding project, the more easily these pitfalls can be avoided or corrected with minimal impact. Developing systematic, well-defined procedures for the project, and including them in a manual distributed to all project participants will help keep these problems to a minimum.

Another problem that libraries have encountered is library users' misperceptions concerning the purpose of barcode labels. It is not uncommon for library users to assume that the barcode labels work in conjunction with the library's security system, and for unscrupulous individuals to deface or remove barcode labels, assuming that this will deactivate the "target" for the security system. Publicity detailing what the barcodes are and how they will be used in the new automated circulation system should help correct this misunderstanding and reduce or eliminate vandalized barcodes (although it will not eliminate theft by determined individuals).

The barcoding process is not contained within a finite project. Barcoding items in the collection will continue throughout the life of the automated circulation system. New acquisitions and items that have been bound or repaired will all require barcoding as part of their normal processing. In addition to developing procedures for the major barcoding initiative that will precede the implementation of the automated circulation system, procedures will also need to be developed for the on-going barcoding that will be required after the new system is operational. In addition, procedures will be needed to process unbarcoded items that turn up at circulation service desks and require immediate attention. This is especially critical if the library does not plan to have the circulating collection completely barcoded by the time the new automated circulation system is activated. Procedures for applying barcode labels and creating the accompanying system records must be developed for every situation that service desk staff are likely to encounter. These procedures should be detailed in a readily-accessible circulation policies and procedures manual. Since most of these unbarcoded items will come to the attention of circulation service desk staff as a result of a library user asking to check out the item, the procedures should be liberal enough to allow library users to charge these items out during all hours the circulation service desk is open, no matter who is staffing the desk or what system functions they have been authorized to perform. For those staff who are not authorized to create system records, an alternative procedure that is transparent to library users must be devised.

CREATING A PATRON RECORD DATABASE

To perform its most basic function, that of linking an item in the library collection to information about the individual to whom it is charged, the automated circulation system requires a database of individual patron records. Each patron record should include information about that individual library user that is useful or appropriate for tracking circulation activities. There are three ways to create a patron record database:

1. Create a Patron Record Database from Scratch

Using this approach, library staff enter into the system the required information for each library user, one record at a time. These records may be batched and created systematically prior to the implementation of the new automated circulation system, or they may be created individually on an as-needed basis once the system is operational.

2. Import a Patron Record Database from Another Source

If other offices within the agency, institution, or organization have created databases that include the information required for the automated circulation system patron database (such as databases that compile information for student registration, identification cards, or human resources/personnel activities), it may be possible to import, via data tapes or disks, information from these databases into the system that will be used by the library. Such transfers are accomplished by utilizing an interface program that will extract the pertinent data in these external files and adapt them to the record format required by the automated circulation system.

3. Compile a Patron Record Database by Combining Staff-Created and Imported Records

Even if the patron record database will be created from data imported into the library database from other external databases, a supplemental infusion of records created by library staff will probably be needed. If the library is part of a large institution or organization, in all likelihood there will be gaps in the imported database(s) that the library must fill. For example, an academic library may include evening students or alumni of the institution among authorized borrowers, yet individuals within these groups may not have records in the campus database(s) imported to create the patron database. A corporate library that imports its database from the company's Human Resources Office may find that records for non-U.S. or short-term contract employees are missing. In addition, patron records will need to be created for individual library units or activities. These records, sometimes referred to as "pseudo" patron records, allow libraries to use the automated circulation system to "charge" items to library units (such as technical processing, interlibrary loan, or document delivery units) or library activities (such as binding or repair). Using the automated circulation system to track items within these areas or activities provides accurate, up-to-date information that is available online immediately, generates item availability or other special messages in the online public catalog, and takes advantage of the automatic features of the circulation system such as the production of overdue notices. Pseudo patron records may be fundamental to transaction record-keeping within document delivery and interlibrary loan service units.

INFORMATION IN PATRON RECORDS

The first step in creating a patron record database is the same as the first step in creating a bibliographic record database. Begin by analyzing the requirements of the new automated circulation system, as well as the information requirements of the library, in order to determine what information should be contained in patron records. Enough information should be included so that library staff can perform their jobs, the system can do its work in processing correct, informative notices and bills for library users, and aggregated statistical reports can be compiled for library managers, administrators, and external reporting agencies. However, exercise extreme caution when including any information in patron records beyond that which is necessary for library staff or the automated circulation system to do their jobs. Avoid including information about individual library users that would be interesting to have but which is unnecessary for circulation functions. Extraneous information in patron records potentially increases the variety of ways that private information about individuals may be misused, thus violating state and/or federal laws.

There are a number of sensitive issues concerning information that may be included in patron records. Some information that may be included routinely, such as a Social Security number, is protected information according to federal law and should not be released under any circumstances. The protected status of other information included in patron records, such as addresses, varies from state to state according to the laws enacted in that state. Instead of trying to sort through which information is public and which is private, it is wise to treat all information included in a patron record as private, protected information. All library staff who have access to individual patron records should be thoroughly indoctrinated on the importance of treating this personal data as confidential information. Confidential information in a patron record includes personal information about a library user (address, phone number, Social Security number, etc.) as well as any record of library activities (past or present fines, items charged, database searches done, keys assigned, rooms rented, etc.) that are included in an individual's record. Library policy should state unequivocally that no information in a patron record should be released to anyone except to the patron who "owns" the record after he or she has provided library staff with an appropriate form of identification, preferably one that includes a photograph. Sanctions should be devised and supported by library administration to ensure the discipline and possible termination of staff abusing the use of this privileged information.

CREATING A PATRON RECORD DATABASE FROM SCRATCH

Most libraries build patron record databases by having library staff key in data for individual patron records.[15] A library user fills out an application form, and an authorized staff member enters the information from the form into the system. A library card, complete with barcode, is handed to the library user after the barcode number from the card has been entered in the newly-created patron record. Although the process for creating patron records this way is a simple one, it may be time-consuming to construct an entire patron record database in this fashion if the library has a large clientele.

Library staff can enter patron records on an as-needed basis as library users approach the circulation service desk, but this is practical on a mass scale only in those libraries experiencing a relatively low volume of circulation activity. A more workable alternative is to encourage library users to "register" with the library prior to the implementation of the new circulation system. Flyers posted within and outside the library, bookmarks that are tucked into charged items, mailings, and advertisements included in newsletters or newspapers can be used to announce the need for library users to register with the library in order to borrow library materials. Any publicity should provide clear instructions for the registration process and the names and phone numbers of individuals who may be contacted for further information. In addition, most of these mediums can also include registration forms that can be filled out in advance and mailed to the library or dropped into a registration box within the library. The registration process should be made as easy as possible for library users, both to encourage them to register and to provide them with a good initial impression of the new system. For ease of data entry, the application form should mirror the format of the online patron record as closely as possible. With the many graphics capabilities that exist today, a form that consists of an enlarged, polished version of a "screen dump" is possible (see Fig. 6-2). Application forms can be batched and the data entered systematically into the patron record database by library staff. Or, staff can enter a brief record with only essential information into the system as the library user waits, filling in the details at a later time. If this approach will be used, it is important to make sure staff are especially conscientious about following up on these incomplete records. In any case, a registration period will provide library staff with some control over scheduling the additional workload that will be generated by the creation of patron records.

IMPORTING A PATRON RECORD DATABASE FROM ANOTHER SOURCE

The need for library staff to key in individual patron records will be reduced considerably if information from databases external to the library can be imported to create the major portion of the patron record database. Systems staff from the library or computer center will need to write an interface program to effect this transfer of data. The interface program should transfer essential information from the source database to the patron record database in a format that conforms to that required by library patron records. It should be written so that the resulting patron records require little or no correction before they are available for use within the new automated circulation system. The interface program should also prohibit the transfer of any extraneous information from the source database to the patron record database. Although a carefully written interface program will eliminate major problems with the transfer of external data into the patron record database, the process of transferring information from data tapes to another system is rarely error-free. An individual from the library staff should

FIGURE 6-2 NOTIS Patron Record

```
  LPTF SAME                                            00000000
                                      DISPLAY PATRON RECORD    A304
NAME:                                    CREATED:        01/13/94
SOC SEC NBR:              PAT GRPS:      UPDATED:        none
NOTE:                                    OWES:             $0.00
    TF LIBRARY TRANSACTION FILE SUBRECORD:
       ORG'N ID:                         SOURCE:
       DEPARTMENT:                        CREATED:       none
       FINES F'GVN:     0      RECALLED ITEMS:    0  UPDATED:       none
       OVERRIDE ADDRESS TYPE:   EXPIRES:    indef  DELETE:        indef
       PATR CODE 1:            PATR CODE 2:
       LUIS MESSGE:
       PATRON ID:                        ID BEGINS:      01/13/94
         CATEGORY:                       ID EXPIRES:     01/13/95
        ·ITEMS CHRGD:    0      OVERDUE:         0   ID DELETE:      indef
         ID STATUS:   active   SOURCE:              LAST CHARGE:    none
  ADDRESS INFORMATION:          USE ADDRESSES FROM PATRON GROUP:
                                          UPDATED:        none
                                          VALID:          01/13/94
                                          INVALID:        01/13/95
                                          DELETE:         indef
       ZIP CODE:              MAIL:       TYPE:
       TELEPHONE:                         SOURCE:
```

FIGURE 6-2 (continued) Sample Patron Record Data Entry Form

Clip Barcode Here

Temporary Patron Record

NAME:
SOC SEC NBR: PAT GRPS: CREATED:
NOTE: UPDATED:
TF Library Transaction File Subrecord: OWES:
  ORG'N ID: SOURCE:
  DEPARTMENT: CREATED:
  FINES F'GVN: RECALLED ITEMS: UPDATED:
  OVERRIDE ADDRESS TYPE: EXPIRES: DELETE:
  PATR CODE 1:   PATR CODE 2:
  LUIS MESSGE:
PATRON ID: **ID BEGINS:**
  CATEGORY: **ID EXPIRES:**
  ITEMS CHRGD: OVERDUE: ID DELETE:
  ID STATUS: SOURCE: LAST CHARGE:
ADDRESS INFORMATION: Use Addresses from
                                 Patron Group:
                                                                  UPDATED:
                                                                  VALID:
                                                                  INVALID:
                                                                  DELETE:
ZIP CODE: MAIL: TYPE:
TELEPHONE: SOURCE:

If above address is temporary, indicate the permanent address below:

ADDRESS INFORMATION: UPDATED:
                                                                  VALID:
                                                                  INVALID:
                                                                  DELETE:
                                                                  TYPE:
ZIP CODE: MAIL: SOURCE:
TELEPHONE:

Attach any documentation to the back of this form:

Send completed forms to:

be assigned to monitor the tapeloads, and be authorized to correct errors and edit records as necessary.

Tapeloading data from one system to another is a convenient way to create a patron database, but it is not without its problems. Consider the timeliness of the data being imported. If it takes weeks for new data to be entered into the source database, and weeks more to finally import that data into the patron record database, the delay may prove counterproductive if library staff are required to key in corrections or even entire records to cope with this delay in accessing up-to-date information. If the information in the source database is not current when it is loaded into the patron record database, or is not updated frequently enough for library staff to accurately determine individual library users' borrowing privileges, service desk scenarios will develop that are frustrating for both library staff and users.

Another issue to consider is the comprehensiveness of the source database. Does it include all, or least a majority, of the users to whom the library lends? If significant sectors of the user population are missing (for instance, alumni or evening students within academic library user groups, or contract employees within corporate library user groups), library staff may spend a significant amount of time entering individual patron records on an as-needed basis, losing the control and convenience a library-planned registration period can offer.

In addition, the interface program may be difficult to write. It may be impossible to write a program that will translate all of the information in the source database into language the automated circulation system can understand. Important data may not transfer to patron records and may need to be entered using an alternative method. Bear in mind that the interface program will not be able to supply the patron record database with data not included in the source database.

One last factor to consider may be a very important one in determining whether or not to import the patron record database from another source. In general, only a small portion of the records in imported databases will belong to actual library users. Once the best-possible interface program has been written and information is being transferred from the source database to the patron record database, is an inordinate amount of staff time being spent troubleshooting tapeloads and correcting errors, given the percentage of actual library users represented by the tapeloads? If so, perhaps the tapeloading concept should be reconsidered.

BORROWING CARDS FOR LIBRARY USERS

Just as library materials will have barcodes, so will library users. A quickly-accessible library user barcode will most likely be placed on the card that the user will present to a circulation desk attendant when checking out library materials. For libraries in which patron records will be manually entered into the system, barcoded library cards can be generated when the data on registration applications are entered into the system (see Fig. 6-3). If the registration forms and barcoded library cards are not processed while library users wait, but are batched and entered at the convenience of library staff, cards can either be mailed directly to library users or held at the circulation service desk for pick-up the next time the individual enters the library. In larger library systems where there are many circulation service desks, a post card can be sent to each library user announcing the availability of their library card at a specific library location. Alternatively, to avoid complicating the application process any more than necessary, it may be desirable to create a special service area where library staff can process application forms as they are received and immediately distribute cards.

Special library cards may not be necessary if the institution or organization issues barcoded identification cards to individuals who will need to borrow library materials. If the barcodes on the identification cards are compatible with the barcode requirements of the new automated circulation system, the barcode from the identification card may be entered into the patron record either manually or via tapeloaded data. If the barcodes on the identification cards are incompatible with the requirements of the new automated circulation system, or if the identification cards have no barcodes at all, it still may be possible to use them as library cards if there is room for library staff to affix barcodes to the cards. Barring the availability of institutional or organizational identification cards, this method might also work with alternative forms of identification, such as the back of an individual's drivers license. Whether the library generates its own cards or is able to use existing identification cards, patron records will still need to be entered into the patron record database.

FIGURE 6-3 A Sample Borrowing Card

UNIVERSITY OF MINNESOTA—TWIN CITIES
LIBRARIES BORROWERS CARD

This card is issued to _____

for _____ loan privileges.

Expires _____

Issued by _____

_____ Library

UNIVERSITY OF MINNESOTA

2 00T0 000 025 061 X

This card provides borrowing privileges at the University of Minnesota—Twin Cities campus libraries, including the Law Library.

The card holder is responsible for abiding by established library policies, and prompt payment of any charges incurred by late return, damage, or lost library material.

RETURN LOST CARDS TO: **Circulation Unit**
Wilson Library
309 19th Ave. S.
University of Minnesota
Minneapolis, MN 55455

CONVERTING EXISTING CIRCULATION RECORDS

At the start-up of the new automated circulation system, current circulation information will still exist in circulation files created under the previous circulation system. Although the data in these files are not essential for the new automated circulation system to perform its function, this information *is* essential to the currency and accuracy of the data provided by the new system. Once the automated circulation system is activated and information about the circulation status of individual items is available to the public via the public catalog, library users will assume that the circulation status of every library item is included in the system. They will be puzzled to learn that even though the library has a wonderful automated circulation system, library staff still must consult manual or other system files to determine an item's circulation status. Given the service element involved, serious consideration should be given to entering the records from these old files into the new system. Misleading information in the public catalog, the need for staff to check a number of files to answer a simple circulation question, and the staff time and energy that must be diverted from other activities in order to run two systems side-by-side for any length of time can all be minimized by mounting a conversion project for these files. In addition, the library will want to take advantage of the automated features of the system, such as the printing of notices, the processing of fines, and the printing of bills for all of its transactions, old and new, as soon as possible.

There are three ways to handle existing manual circulation files:

1. Elimination of Files by Attrition

If the files are small, and loan periods short, the library can choose not to mount a conversion project, and instead wait for attrition (items coming due, bills being paid, etc.) to eliminate the existing files. These files will disappear gradually as items are returned and bills are paid. This may work quite well in smaller circulation units where there is a relatively low volume of activity. However, there will be no accounting in the automated system for any records that are not removed from the files within a reasonable time period, for instance, records of long-term loans or missing items.

2. Immediate Conversion of All Existing Files

A project to convert all manual circulation files can begin as soon as it is possible to enter records into the production region of the new automated circulation system. Unless loan periods are very long, or the majority of records in the file are not expected to be closed any time soon, the library may waste a good deal of staff energy with this approach. Of particular concern are units with a high volume of circulation activity that have resulted in very large files. Library staff may spend an inordinate amount of time converting open charge records that will come due within a very short time period, perhaps a few weeks after the system is activated.

3. Combined Attrition and Conversion of Existing Files

The optimal solution is a combination of attrition and conversion of existing circulation files. Depending on the size of the unit and its files, the period selected for attrition may range from one day to two months from the time it is possible to begin entering records into the production region of the new automated circulation system. Once that period and the due dates within it have expired and the records have been processed, a conversion project can begin with the remaining records. The library could also begin a conversion project right away, beginning with the records expected to remain in the files the longest (e.g., records for "lost" items, or long-term loans). The project could work toward the records expected to disappear most quickly, saving the shortest-term loans' records for last. This approach allows library staff to begin converting records right away, perhaps prior to the official start-up date, yet allows for some natural decrease in the total number of records requiring conversion. This approach, especially if it is possible to begin prior to the official start-up date of the system, also allows staff to practice what they've learned in training sessions. The conversion of existing circulation records provides staff with an excellent opportunity to handle both routine and exceptional situations in a non-threatening environment. Staff are able to work at their own pace without worrying that users are waiting or lines forming.

Problem situations will arise when converting manual circulation records to machine-readable formats. Records for items or library users recorded in the manual files will be missing from the item and patron record databases. In larger libraries, a number of library users may share the same name and be indistinguishable from one another with the information provided in existing files. A pilot project will help identify these and other potential problem situations. A pilot project will also help determine the policies and procedures that will need to be developed to effectively resolve these and other problem situations. All policies and procedures should be detailed in the circulation procedure manual.

If the library is moving from one automated circulation system to another, transferring the circulation records from the old automated circulation system to the new one should not involve the same degree of onerous data entry as the process to convert manual circulation files to machine-readable form. Library systems staff or staff within the computer center may be able to develop an interface program that will allow a transfer process similar to that used to import data for the patron database.

Although another conversion project will not sound terribly attractive after working through the details to enter information into item and patron record databases, converting existing circulation records is simpler and less expensive than converting the item and patron records. It is also well worth the short-term staff effort since it allows the automated system to take over management and maintenance of the circulation files as soon as possible.

REFERENCES

1. Pat Barkalow, "Conversion of Files for Circulation Control," *Journal of Library Automation* 12 (September 1979): 209.
2. Michael J. Bruer, "The Public Relations Component of Circulation System Implementation," *Journal of Library Automation* 12 (September 1979): 215.
3. Ibid., pp. 210, 213.
4. Richard W. Boss and Judy McQueen, "Automated Circulation Control Systems," *Library Technology Reports* 18 (March/April 1982): 152.
5. Richard W. Boss, *The Library Manager's Guide to Automation,* (Boston, MA: G. K. Hall & Co., 1979): 57.
6. Bruer, "The Public Relations Component of Circulation System Implementation," p. 215.
7. Adapted from Boss, *The Library Manager's Guide to Automation,* p. 57.
8. John Corbin, *Developing Computer-Based Library Systems* (Phoenix, AZ: Oryx Press, 1981): 102.
9. Ibid., pp. 102-3.
10. Association of Research Libraries, Systems and Procedures Exchange Center, *Barcoding of Collections in ARL Libraries,* SPEC Kit #124 (Washington, D.C.: Association of Research Libraries, Office of Management Studies, Systems and Procedures Exchange Center, May 1986): 2.

11. Erwin Rahn, "Bar Codes for Libraries," *Library Hi Tech* 2 (1984): 73.
12. Ibid.
13. Boss, *The Library Manager's Guide to Automation,* pp. 14-15.
14. Ibid.
15. Richard W. Boss, *The Library Manager's Guide to Automation,* Third Edition (Boston, MA: G. K. Hall & Co., 1990): 9.

7 BACKING UP SYSTEM FILES AND FUNCTIONS

System failures can be prompted by a number of circumstances, among them hardware failures, software failures, communication link failures, loss of electricity, natural disasters, and, on occasion, human error. The system may be down for minutes or it may be down for days. A system failure could result in nothing more than the temporary and inconvenient inaccessibility of the automated circulation system. It could also result in a more serious, prolonged downtime, involving reconstructing data files that have been destroyed. Fortunately, statistics indicate that the typical system is 98 percent reliable.[1] However, since the automated circulation system will be in almost continuous use once it is implemented, an alternative system, additional copies of data files, and a set of procedures relevant to system downtimes will be needed for the two to five percent of the time that the system will be unavailable.

BACKING UP THE SYSTEM FILES

Most modern individuals understand the importance of backing up personal computer files and software programs. The need for back-up files is no different, and perhaps even more crucial, with a large automated circulation system. Certain files in the system should be copied on a regular basis as part of the system's standard operating procedure. Depending on how frequently the data changes and how much computer time is available, it is critical that copies be made of important files such as the circulation transaction file, the circulation history file, the patron record file, and the bibliographic database with its item records. The circulation transaction file (a record of currently charged items) and the circulation history file (a record of all completed circulation transactions, such as items that have been discharged) should be backed up daily with additional, up-to-date copies. The bibliographic and patron record files can be backed up less frequently with copies made once a week.

It is serious enough if a day or two of data entry in a bibliographic file has been lost and must be duplicated by re-keying all the records that were entered during that period. However, losing a day or two of circulation transactions is an entirely different type of crisis. This type of lost data is virtually impossible to recreate. In addition, losing records for charged and discharged items, bills paid, and recalls and holds placed creates a long list of potential public relations disasters and service nightmares. Worst-case scenarios are not always avoidable, but backing up system files on a regular basis will go a long way toward avoiding major disasters.

BACK-UP SYSTEMS AND PROCEDURES

For those times when the automated circulation system will be inaccessible, a back-up system should be available so that uninterrupted service can be provided to library users. The alternative system, and procedures for activating and using it, should be appropriate for any length of down time, whether the system is down for two hours or two days. Ideally, the alternative system and procedures both should be: 1) simple to activate, 2) easy to use (mirroring the automated system as much as possible), and 3) allow for efficient entry of the transactions recorded during the downtime once the automated system is operational again.

The alternative system and procedures should subject library staff and users to a minimum of inconvenience. It won't matter to either library staff or users what the cause of the downtime is, be it an electrical failure in the building, a broken telecommunications link between the library and the main computer, or a malfunctioning of the main computer. It makes little difference to them whether the system is down in just one library or the whole library system. The reasons for the downtime are relatively insignificant. If staff or library users are unable to access the system from wherever they happen to be at that moment, from their perspective the "system" is down.[2] If the alternative system and procedures are well-conceived, library users may not even notice that the system is down. For library staff, however, system downtime is an inconvenience. A back-up system and procedures that follow the three guidelines mentioned above will keep that inconvenience to a minimum.

SELECTING A BACK-UP METHOD

There are a number of back-up alternatives for an automated circulation system, each with its own shortcomings. Tape cassettes that attach to a regular terminal are unreliable, bubble memory devices don't have a large enough capacity, and portable, battery-operated units are fragile, requiring frequent and expensive repairs.[3] Another option, running a back-up program on a personal computer, has proven to be a more successful back-up alternative. Over 80 percent of libraries using automated circulation systems are now using personal computers as a system back-up option—either purchasing vendor-supplied back-up options for their systems or creating their own home-grown programs.[4] Libraries using personal computers in circulation service areas will increase the usefulness of that workstation hardware configuration by utilizing the capabilities of these computer terminals for back-up during system downtimes. Generally, personal computer-based back-up systems mimic the "real" system. They allow library staff to record transaction data while the automated circulation system is down and transfer that data from the back-up program to the automated circulation system once the system is operational again.

A back-up system may prove to be a good investment beyond simply serving as an alternative system for automated circulation system downtimes. At some institutions, back-up programs also are being used as effective means for inventory control.[5] If this kind of dual purpose is planned, portability of the equipment on which the back-up program will run will be a factor to consider.

USING A PERSONAL COMPUTER PROGRAM FOR BACK-UP

If a back-up program on a personal computer is going to serve as the alternative for system downtimes, there will need to be at least one personal computer on which the program may be run at each service desk. If library materials continue to be discharged while the system is down rather than delaying the discharging process until the system is once again operational, at least one personal computer will be needed in each area where materials will be discharged. As an alternative, consider instituting a policy that states that no library materials will be discharged using the back-up program when the automated circulation system is down for less than one working day. Since most automated circulation systems allow for back-dating when discharging library materials, library users can still be credited the next day with returning their materials during the day and time of the system outage. Unlike the situation where a patron wants to charge an item and leave the library, returned materials can remain in the staff work area and be discharged once the system is operational again. By not using the back-up program for discharges during short system outages, charged items are discharged directly through the automated circulation system once it is operational again. Avoiding the two-step process of recording the information in the back-up program and then entering it into the automated circulation system at a later time decreases the chances for data entry errors or lost transactions. For longer downtimes, consider how quickly returned materials are likely to accumulate. It might be better to take a chance on lost transactions or data entry errors than to let library materials pile up and become seriously backlogged. A backlog can create an uneven, burdensome workflow for circulation staff, and increase the chance that items will be misplaced before they are discharged. A backlog also means that larger quantities of library materials will remain unshelved and inaccessible to library users.

Most personal computer back-up programs function the same way as automated circulation systems (i.e., they require that the barcode on a library user's identification card be scanned into the computer followed by a scan of the item barcode). The information provided by the back-up program subsequent to scanning a barcode can be quite useful, depending on what is coded into the string of characters represented by the barcode. For instance, the system may be able to display the patron category of the library user to assist library staff in assigning an appropriate due date.

Some personal computer back-up programs will record the transaction data on a computer file. This file can then be read into the automated circulation system when it is once again operational. Other programs will provide a printout of patron and item barcodes that represent individual circulation transactions (see Fig. 7-1). These barcodes can then be scanned, transaction by transaction, into the automated circulation system.

LIMITATIONS OF THE BACK-UP PROGRAM

A back-up system that truly mirrors the automated system needs complete and up-to-date item and patron records, and should be capable of producing messages and flags for blocks, recalls, holds, and the like. Although this would ensure a high degree of accuracy during system downtimes, the cost to produce and regularly up-

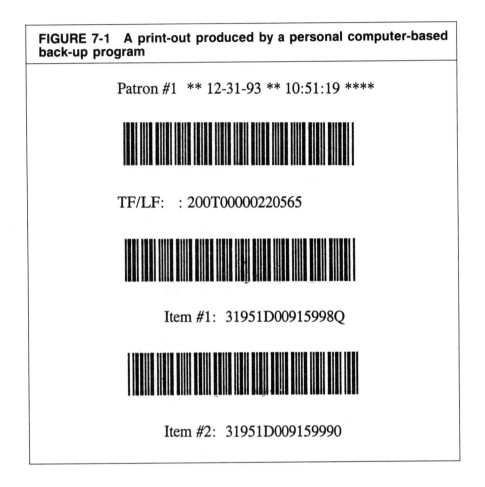

FIGURE 7-1   A print-out produced by a personal computer-based back-up program

Patron #1 ** 12-31-93 ** 10:51:19 ****

TF/LF: : 200T00000220565

Item #1: 31951D00915998Q

Item #2: 31951D009159990

date such a system, tantamount to running two systems side-by-side, would be prohibitive. Also, given the number of problem situations likely to arise during a system outage, the costs of producing the system would greatly outweigh the advantages of catching the relatively infrequent problem transaction. Lacking such an extensive back-up system means that library staff will not have access to patron records during system outages, nor will they be able to determine whether or not a library user does indeed have current borrowing privileges. In addition, it will not be possible for staff to determine if a discharged item should be placed on the hold or recall shelf, or routed to another unit in the library. These messages and flags will not appear when transactions are recorded in the back-up program, however they *will* appear when the data from the back-up system is read into the automated circulation system. Procedures for handling these situations will need to be identified and detailed for library staff.

Since the back-up system will be limited in terms of what it can provide for transactions beyond routine charges or discharges, consider carefully the process that will be used to read the circulation data recorded by the back-up program into the automated circulation system. Although some personal computer programs will allow library staff to simply give a command to play back and read in all the back-up data, problems will arise when the system encounters non-routine transactions, such as an item that has been recalled or a patron whose borrowing privileges are blocked. A back-up program that provides a data file should include a feature that flags non-routine transactions as they are being read into the automated circulation system, or better yet, transaction-by-transaction processing of the data that will allow staff to review the data and intervene as necessary. The data entry process will need to be monitored by a staff member authorized to override system-supplied due dates, blocks, recalls, and holds. Even seemingly routine transactions may become problematic. For instance, if the back-up program has no way of identifying the patron category of each library user, one due date may be assigned using the back-up program, and another when the data is read into the automated circulation system (e.g., an undergraduate student loan of six weeks in one system, and a graduate student loan of ten weeks in another). Public relations difficulties may ensue if the loan period assigned using the back-up program is a longer loan period than the one the automated circulation system will automatically assign when the back-up transactions are read into the system. This can be forestalled by utilizing a program that offers transaction-by-transaction entry of data. The monitor will also need to acknowledge and adjust flags or messages as they appear. Setting aside discharged items that must be placed on the hold shelf or routed to another library will be part of the monitoring process. A program that provides a printout of patron and item barcodes is not as quick or simple a method for data entry, however, it does by its nature allow for transaction-by-transaction review during the data entry process.

Personal computer-based back-up programs are an improvement over the other electronic options listed earlier. They are certainly a major advance from the "Parker-Hammermill" method of writing down the transaction information on a piece of paper or a form.[6] Manual methods may be necessary to supplement both the regular and back-up system when both are down due to electrical failure. Care should be taken that staff know exactly what information to record in such circumstances and how important it is that the information be legible, accurate, and complete. Staff will need to take special care to ensure that the data entered into the automated circulation system is complete and accurate. Preprinted forms for recording the data during these occasions make this process a more efficient one.

PURCHASING/WRITING A PERSONAL COMPUTER BACK-UP SYSTEM

When purchasing or writing a personal computer back-up system, there are six basic requirements that the system should meet:[7]

1. Quick and easy start-up.
2. Electronic input of barcodes.
3. Check-digit calculation for each barcode (a message should display to the terminal operator if the check digit is incorrect).
4. System prompts that mirror those in the automated system.
5. Capacity to store 1,000 to 5,000 transactions (if the data will be saved in a computer file).
6. Simple transfer of data to the automated circulation system, either by scanning barcodes from a printout or loading a computerized file of transactions.

Back-up systems generally require a minimal investment to prepare or purchase. Excluding the cost of the personal computers (which will be ordered as part of the automated circulation system hardware requirements), a back-up program and documentation to support it can generally be purchased or written for under $1,000. A small investment, indeed, for the benefits a computer-based back-up system will provide.

REFERENCES

1. Richard W. Boss, *The Library Manager's Guide to Automation,* Third Edition (Boston, MA: G. K. Hall & Co., 1990): 143.
2. Joseph R. Matthews, "20 Q's & A's on Automated Integrated Library Systems," *Journal of Academic Librarianship* 13 (June 1982): 369.
3. Boss, *The Library Manager's Guide to Automation*, p. 118.
4. Ibid.

5. Edward A. Stockey, "The Design of a Backup for an Online Circulation System at Indiana State University," *Library Hi Tech News* 46 (February 1988): 2.

6. Credit for the appellation, "Parker-Hammermill System," belongs to Bill Divens (aka, "Rustbelt Bill" on the NOTIS-L listserv), Head of Access Services at the University of Pittsburgh.

7. Adapted from, Edward A. Stockey, "The Design of a Backup for an Online Circulation System at Indiana State University," pp. 2-3.

8 WORKING WITH CIRCULATION POLICIES AND PROCEDURES

Whether the library is automating circulation activities for the first time, or switching from one automated circulation system to another, current circulation policies and procedures will need to be reviewed in light of the new automated circulation system. Circulation policies provide the rules and regulations that govern circulation activities. Careful examination of circulation policies is especially important since many will be incorporated into the new automated circulation system parameters, and thus dictate the way the system will perform its automatic functions. The standardized routines and activities that support circulation policies are circulation procedures. Circulation procedures define in detail, usually step-by-step, how routine and non-routine circulation transactions will be handled, whether or not the system will be used for the transaction, and if the system is used, and if an override of its automatic functions is necessary, how this will be accomplished. A comprehensive accounting of both circulation policies and procedures should be documented in the circulation manual.

Close scrutiny of existing policies and procedures, and thoughtful reflection on the basic premise underlying each policy or procedure, will help determine what revisions are necessary to accommodate the requirements of the new system yet maintain services that meet the needs of library users.

EXAMINING CURRENT POLICIES AND PROCEDURES

Tradition has always played a large role in circulation activities. With the implementation of a new automated circulation system, the library is afforded the opportunity to remove "the blinders of tradition" and use the opportunity as a catalyst for change.[1] As the library moves from a manual circulation system that restricts service options to a sophisticated, flexible automated system that offers expanded service potential, circulation services can be tailored more to library users' needs and less to the restrictions imposed by the system being replaced. This presents an opportunity to examine library policies and procedures in light of what would best serve the user community. New or revised policies and procedures can be the result of a thoughtful analysis of user needs rather than a product of a "we've-always-done-it-that-way" mindset. However, change for the sake of change (i.e., arbitrarily changing policies and procedures merely because the library is changing circulation systems) is not advised. Much wiser are informed changes that are made at a time when opportunity allows for change as a logical, natural step in the course of events.

Whether current policies and procedures were developed decades ago to fit a manual circulation system or have been revised within recent years to accommodate the implementation of a previous automated circulation system, in all likelihood the new system will have different requirements and library staff will be required to interact with it in a manner different from that required by the old system. Prior to making any changes, service requirements of the various units within the library, as well as those of library users, will need to be considered and weighed against conditions that will allow the new system to perform at its most efficient. Questions to ask as current policies and procedures are reviewed include the following:

1. What does it cost to maintain the policy or procedure at its current level?
2. What costs or savings would be realized by revising or eliminating the policy or procedure?
3. Does the activity need to be completed with the same level of attention and detail (i.e., can the procedure be pared down or even eliminated completely?)?
4. If the activity is completed with a lesser degree of accuracy, what consequences would result?
5. What consequences would result from outright elimination of the policy or procedure?
6. Is the policy or procedure logical and justifiable, or has it become merely a tradition, without clear meaning, over the years?
7. What role does this policy or procedure play in positive public relations with library users? How would this relationship be impacted if the activity was changed or eliminated?

8. What comfort factor is inherent in this activity for library staff? Will revising or eliminating the activity increase staff members' anxiety level in adjusting to a new system?

These questions will provide an excellent starting point for group discussion of the revisions that are needed to adapt existing policies and procedures to the new automated circulation system.

THE IMPACT OF A SHARED DATABASE

If this is the first automated circulation system that the library has implemented, it is important that all staff, in particular those individuals who will be reviewing circulation policies and procedures, understand that the new automated circulation system will be shared by staff throughout the library. Depending on the size of the library, this may mean that staff in one circulation area and one or two technical service units will be using the system. It may also mean that many units in a number of different libraries within the organization will be sharing the system and contributing to a common database. Any changes in the policies or procedures that will be used in this shared system will have repercussions throughout the entire library. Individual units accustomed to developing their own ad hoc policies and procedures will no longer be able to do so. Consultation with others in the library organization will, of necessity, precede most policy or procedural changes. The need to carefully consider whether or not specific actions on their part will have system-wide implications is one of the most difficult, yet most important, adjustments that staff in formerly autonomous units will make. However, this decrease in autonomy does not mean that units cannot implement any individualistic policies or procedures. It simply means that careful thought and discussion within an advisory group appointed to review such issues should precede any policy or procedure changes, whether those changes are intended to address issues specific to an individual library unit or to the library as a whole. While there is still room for individuality via system parameters, staff need to be aware of what types of actions are likely to have system-wide consequences. Initially, this may not be easy to identify, since staff will still be learning what the new system will and will not do.

Specifically, some areas where policy or procedural decisions are likely to produce system-wide consequences include: 1) parameters set for loan periods, fine rates, or renewal limits; 2) procedures that will be used to convert manual circulation records to a machine-readable format; and, 3) acceptable formats for text or codes in patron or item records. Unit-to-unit differences may be possible in all areas except the last—depending on the library and the services required by library users. For instance, it may be possible to implement several loan periods for periodicals within different libraries in the organization or within different collections in the library, depending on the use patterns exhibited by library users within different disciplines. However, allowing each unit to develop its own set of codes for use in system records will inhibit consistent interpretation of these records by staff throughout the library. A shared database that includes a crazy quilt of policies and data entry procedures is confusing at best, dysfunctional at worst.

DEVELOPING CIRCULATION POLICIES AND PROCEDURES

During the process of reviewing existing policies and procedures, it will become evident that additional policies and procedures must be created to address situations that were not encountered using the existing circulation system. Whether revising old policies and procedures or creating entirely new ones, it is important to remember that automated systems are designed to handle the routine. Automated circulation systems, in particular, do not deal with exceptions to routine very well. Policies that will be incorporated into system parameters or functions should reflect the majority of circulation transactions likely to be handled by the automated circulation system, rather than the exceptions that will arise less frequently. Basing system policies on a small number of infrequent, exceptional circumstances means that routine transactions will become exceptional as far as the system is concerned, and library staff will spend an inordinate amount of time overriding system functions. The convenience and efficiencies of an automated circulation system will be lost as staff constantly override the automatic functions the system should be providing. Undermining the potential efficiencies of the new system in this manner may cause library staff and users to perceive, incorrectly, that the system is a failure. In such a situation, it is the use of the system, not the system itself, that is unsuccessful.

Although circulation policies and the automated circulation system parameters should be structured to reflect routine circulation transactions, circulation procedures should be developed to reflect both routine and non-routine transactions that circulation units are likely to encounter. For instance, it may be library policy for a library user to present a valid library card at a circulation service desk before library materials will be charged to that individual. What procedures should library staff follow when this routine situation occurs? On the other hand, when a library user doesn't have her or his library card, but wants to charge out library materials, what procedures should circulation staff follow to handle this non-routine situation? Procedures can also be developed to meet routine, long-term needs or short-term, specialized needs. Perhaps in the first few months of system operation, library staff want to determine how accurate the system is in printing overdue notices for library users. For those first few months, a procedure may be developed which incorporates into the normal routine of mailing out these notices a physical check of the library shelves prior to mailing a notice, just to make sure the item has not been returned and reshelved. After the accuracy of the system has been determined to be acceptable, this short-term procedure may be abandoned and a long-term procedure can be developed that allows for the immediate mailing of such notices without first checking the items listed on the notices against items on library shelves.

Although each library will differ with respect to specific system, staff, and user needs, the following areas will need to be reviewed prior to adopting any policies or procedures for use under the new system. The questions listed under each area should help prompt group discussion. Priorities will vary from library to library, therefore, the following issues are listed in random, rather than priority order.

Loan Codes

How will loan periods be determined (e.g., by library or collection, item format, item location, and/or patron category)? Will there be a limit on the number of items loaned simultaneously to a single individual? What type of due dates are preferred, many rolling due dates or a few predetermined due dates per quarter?

Deciding what loan periods the library will use may not be a simple issue to resolve, especially if the library includes several formerly autonomous units accustomed to accommodating the diverse needs of their users. Loans may vary from patron group to patron group, as well as from collection to collection, or library to library. In addition, some units may opt for predetermined due dates (perhaps several per quarter) while others find rolling due dates better for distributing unit workloads. Fortunately, many automated circulation systems allow for a great deal of customization in regard to loan period parameters. For most libraries, the issue will not be whether or not the system can handle a diverse array of loan codes, but whether or not it is in the best interests of the library users to establish a uniform loan code throughout the library organization.

Arguments in favor of establishing a uniform loan code center on the user. Proponents will claim library users prefer to have a simple system where one loan code is common to all units in the library or library organization, and individuals are not required to sort out an array of due dates for materials from different libraries. Also, with the new automated circulation system, library users will have a single system from which they will access their circulation information and will perceive "the library" as a single functioning unit rather than many smaller units. A uniform loan code has benefits for library staff as well. Utilizing a single loan code in the system makes it easier to handle any additional software programming that may be necessary to adapt the automated circulation system to the unique needs of the library. A single loan code also simplifies any data entry in or changes to tables in table-driven systems.

On the other hand, arguments in favor of individualizing loan codes in various library units also center on the user. Proponents of this argument will claim that use of library materials varies according to discipline. For instance, users of science or engineering periodicals want the most current information in unbound issues of periodicals to be readily available and may prefer that these issues not leave the library. On the other hand, readers of an underground press publication may not encounter the same competition for the most current issues, and may ask that they be allowed to charge out these issues for a day or two. Older, bound issues of periodicals may circulate for a week, an arrangement which may suit most library users except the researchers in geology who must have access to the original article and its accompanying geologic maps for extended periods of time. Critics of a uniform loan code argue that a "one-size-fits-all" approach will hamper a large sector of researchers whose needs do not fit into a universal loan code.

If the automated circulation system is designed to handle a multitude of loan codes, these individuals will argue, the library should accommodate researchers' needs and not implement a uniform loan code merely for the convenience of library staff.

Arguments for and against a uniform loan code have merit, with the relative weight of one set of arguments against another largely depending on the needs of the user population the library supports. The final decision may not satisfy extremists on either side of the argument, but may incorporate both positions with a uniform loan code for some materials (such as monographs), and individualistic loan codes for others (such as bound or unbound issues of periodicals).

Renewals

How long a renewal period, and how many renewals, will be allowed by patron group, item format and/or item location? How will renewals be accepted (e.g., in person, by phone, by mail, etc.)? Must the physical item be produced before staff will authorize its renewal? Can overdue library items be renewed? If so, will the individual be required to bring in the item prior to staff authorizing its renewal?

Recalls and Holds

Under what circumstances will recalls and holds be allowed? How long will a library user be allowed to retain a charged item before a recall can be placed? How long will an individual have to return an item that has been recalled for another individual's use? What notification will be sent to the individuals (the recaller and the recallee) involved in the recall or hold process? How long will an item remain on the library's "hold" shelf before the next individual is notified of its availability, or it is returned to the stacks? How will the queue be sequenced if more than one individual has asked that the same item be recalled or held?

Circulating Non-Circulating Items

What types of non-circulating items will be allowed to circulate, and under what circumstances? What library unit(s) and/or staff will be allowed to authorize non-routine circulations? What notes, codes or data changes need to be entered into the item record, and who will be authorized to do so? Will all non-routine circulations be handled through the automated circulation system?

Materials that will and will not be circulated through the new automated circulation system will need to be defined. It may be that only circulating items within the collection have been barcoded. If this is the case and it becomes necessary to charge materials that normally do not circulate and have no barcodes or item records in the database, it may be cumbersome to use the automated circulation system to charge these items depending on the library's procedures for handling data entry and barcoding of unbarcoded items at service desks. For items such as maps, music scores, or microforms (any of which may have neither barcodes nor item records), the library may want to avoid the automated system altogether and maintain a small file of manual records for those items that rarely circulate and have loan codes that vary from user to user, depending on the individual's needs. However, if it is desirable to have the circulation information for these or any other normally non-circulating materials available in the automated circulation system so that the system will automatically monitor overdue items, process patron notices, and assess fines, then it may be preferable to circulate these items through the automated circulation system and develop procedures for entering circulation information about these items in the system.

"Courtesy" Services

What "courtesy" services will be provided (i.e., the processing of charges, discharges, renewals, recalls, or holds at units other than the unit that "owns" the item in question)? Which staff members will be authorized to do this in the automated circulation system? How will system overrides, if they should be necessary during a "courtesy" transaction, be handled?

Overdue Items

When will a charged item be considered overdue? Will any notification be sent to library users alerting them that an item's due date is approaching? If advance notification is sent, will it be sent to all patron groups or only selected groups? What type of notification will be sent to library users with overdue materials? Will individuals receive one or more notices? Will library users be required to return overdue items to the library that "owns" the item?

Fines Rates

How will fines be determined (e.g., by item format, item location, patron category, and/or circulation action such as normal overdue, recalled or rush recalled item overdue)? What will the fines rates be for each category?

Sanctions

What sanctions will exist for flagrant abusers of library circulation policies? Will sanctions vary by patron group? What must be done to remove a specific sanction; for instance, will library privileges be restored if an individual pays as much of an outstanding bill as is necessary to reduce it to an acceptable level, or will the individual be required to pay the bill in full before restoration of library privileges? If bills include charges for unreturned items, does the individual have the option of paying for the item, personally buying an identical replacement, or returning the original item in order to reduce the bill?

Sanctions will include restrictions the library wants to impose on delinquent library users. Sanctions could include stopping a library user's borrowing privilege when he or she has a certain number of overdue items, or when a certain dollar amount of outstanding financial obligations has accumulated.

"Lost" or "Missing" Items

When will an overdue item be declared lost? How will this be handled by the automated circulation system? What charges will be assessed a library user for a lost library item? How will returned lost items be handled? Within what time frame will refunds for returned lost items be allowed? How much of the payment (e.g., replacement costs, processing fee, overdue fines) will be refunded? How will uncharged items that cannot be physically located (e.g., missing items) be handled on the system? How, when, and by whom will bibliographic and item records for lost and missing items be withdrawn from the system?

Lists Detailing Individual Library Users' Charges

Under what circumstances will library staff provide a library user with a list detailing items currently charged to her or him? What kind of identification will be required of the individual before the information is released to her or him? How will the library handle phone requests for this information? If proxy cards are a service offered by the library, to whom will information about charges against a faculty proxy card be released?

Faculty "Proxy" Cards

If the library is part of an academic institution and offers faculty the option of using "proxies" to initiate library transactions, under what circumstances and to whom will proxy cards be issued? Will applications for proxy cards be accepted at a special service area? What documentation will be required to authenticate an application for a proxy card?

Library Units as "Pseudo" Patrons

What circulation issues (e.g., overdues, recalls, renewals, loan periods, fine rates, charge/discharge procedures) need to be clarified for "pseudo patrons" like library units (such as document delivery, fee-based services, interlibrary loan, or technical processing units) or functions (such as binding or repair)? What system parameters need to be identified in order to accurately track library items charged to pseudo patrons?

Creation and/or Revision of Patron Records

Under what circumstances will patron records be created or revised for individual library users or library units? Who will be authorized to do this? What data entry standards will be employed, field by field, in these records? What alternative procedures will be available for unauthorized staff who work at service desks and may be called on to perform such activities?

Prior to the implementation of the new automated circulation system, detailed, standardized procedures for data entry into the system's patron records will need to be developed.

Patron Record Tapeloads

If one or more external databases will be imported into the automated circulation system to create the patron record database, when and how will these databases be imported? How will timelags be handled at service desks (e.g., under what circumstances will patron records be added to the library database or modified by library staff prior to the new or revised record's transmittal from the external database(s))? What documentation will be required to authenticate requests for new or modified patron records?

Security of Information in Patron Records

Under what circumstances and to whom will information in individual library users' patron records be released? How will requests for personal information (such as an address, phone number, etc.) be handled? How will requests for circulation information (historical or present charges, bills, etc.) be handled?

It is essential that policies be developed to govern the security of information in patron records, including the confidential information that links charged items to specific library users. Explicit procedures for handling requests for such information will also be needed. Applicable state and federal laws should be consulted before formulating any policies or procedures in this sensitive area. Prior to their implementation, all policies and procedures concerning the security of information in patron records should be reviewed and approved by library administration. As a precautionary measure, it is recommended that the agency, institution, or organization's legal counsel also review these policies and procedures prior to their implementation. Legal counsel should also be consulted to resolve any difficult or controversial issues that may arise during discussion of confidentiality issues. Once the policies and procedures in this area have been developed to conform with any local or federal laws, and have been approved by the library administration and legal counsel, they should also be reviewed and receive formal endorsement and support from any library advisory or governance groups such as student/faculty library committees or library boards.

Creation and/or Revision of Bibliographic or Item Records

Under what circumstances will permanent or temporary bibliographic or item records be created or revised in library units? Who will be authorized to do this? What data entry standards will be employed, field by field, in these records? What alternative procedures will be available for unauthorized staff who work at service desks and may be called on to perform such activities?

Prior to the implementation of the new automated circulation system, detailed, standardized procedures for data entry in the system's bibliographic and item records will need to be developed.

System Overrides

What system parameters or functions is it possible to override, and which will the library utilize? For each type of system override the library decides to utilize, under what circumstances will it be allowed, and who will be authorized to perform it?

Security Profiles/Authorizations

What authorizations are required by the system to allow individual staff to perform certain system functions? Are any authorizations grouped together so that authorization for one function automatically includes authorization for one or more other functions? What must individual staff be authorized to do in order to perform their jobs? What impact will allowing or denying specific authorizations have on a unit's workflow or on its service to library users? What procedural alternatives are available for staff unauthorized to perform certain functions?

Back-Up Program
Under what circumstances will the back-up program be activated? Within what timeframe is it reasonable to expect that all transactions recorded by the back-up program be entered into the automated circulation system? Will any additional identification be required of library users to charge materials while the back-up program is in use? How will overrides and loan code discrepancies be handled when the back-up data is entered into the automated circulation system?

Reserves
Will functions for course reserves be part of the automated circulation system? If so, will those functions be implemented now or at a later date? If not, will items in reserve be charged to reserve, or will their location designations be changed to "reserve?"

Bindery
Will an item sent to the bindery be charged to the bindery or will its location designation be changed to "bindery" in the item record? Will some notation be included to indicate the date the item was sent to the bindery and the estimated return date? What bindery information will appear in the OPAC record for the item?

Creating and Updating System Documentation
How will in-house documentation be reviewed and updated? Who will be responsible for this on-going task? Who will handle distribution of the original documentation and any subsequent revisions? How will it be done?

DEVELOPING DETAILED CIRCULATION PROCEDURES

From its initial discussion to its final inclusion in a circulation procedures manual, the details of each procedure need careful attention. No detail or step should be omitted from any procedure included in the circulation manual. Each procedure should be drafted, test-ed (preferably by someone who knows nothing about the new auto-mated circulation system), and adjusted or corrected as necessary. The testing process is critical since it is easy to overlook a small but crucial step to the procedure when working with such an over-whelming amount of detail, or to make incorrect assumptions or generalizations about the level of skill staff will demonstrate on the new system. In particular, it is very easy for the latter to hap-pen. After the project manager and project team have spent many months testing and experimenting with the system, it is easy to leave out steps that, after many months of practice, have become second nature. The manual will be used by knowledgeable staff, but it will also be used by staff who can't absorb all at once the information presented in training sessions, staff who do not have occasion to use a particular system function frequently, and new staff members for whom the manual is their first introduction to an automated circulation system. Creating a manual of procedures that assume the reader has no knowledge of the system offers the reader a choice of glossing over unnecessary detail or carefully fol-lowing each explicit step depending on that individual's needs.

FINALIZING NEW AND REVISED POLICIES AND PROCEDURES

Any revisions of existing circulation policies or procedures, as well as any newly-created policies or procedures, should be forwarded to all appropriate library committees and to library administra-tion for discussion and approval prior to implementing any changes. In some cases, such as when policy changes pertain to loan codes, sanctions, or security of library records, it is also recommended that approval and support be sought from any library advisory or governance groups. It is critical that a number of groups have in-put on the development and final approval of the loan codes and sanctions that will be used after the new automated circulation sys-tem is implemented. Wide discussion of proposed policies and procedures among staff in circulation units, staff in other library units directly affected by specific policies or procedures, library administrators, and advisory or governance groups provides a firm base for the widespread acceptance of any changes.

Loan codes, fines rates, and sanctions are particularly sensitive areas for library users. If the library has an advisory group, involve those individuals in any discussions on the approval of proposed policies and procedures in these areas. Generally, individual members within such groups are functioning as representatives for other library users and can assist greatly in spotting and correcting troublesome issues as well as gaining widespread acceptance among their constituents for the final policies and procedures. After they have been finalized and approved by all appropriate groups, particulars of the loan code, fines rates, and sanctions for delinquent library users should be widely publicized in library newsletters, library displays, appropriate external publications (including local newspapers), and, if feasible, direct mailings.

AFTER IMPLEMENTATION

Circulation policies and procedures can be developed to meet long-term needs (such as policies and procedures that will be activated when library users come into the library without their library cards and ask to check out library materials) or short-term needs (a procedure for temporarily checking overdue notices against items on the library shelves). No matter how long-term the policy or procedure, however, staff should always be alert to any problems that may indicate a policy or procedure is not working and needs fine-tuning. In addition, the automated circulation system will not be static, but will undergo changes and enhancements throughout its lifetime. User needs will also change as the world of information continues to evolve. As these changes are experienced, policies and procedures may need to change as well. The library's circulation policies and procedures should be viewed as dynamic, reviewed often, and modified as necessary.

REFERENCES

1. Joseph R. Matthews, *Choosing an Automated Library System: A Planning Guide,* (Chicago, IL: American Library Association, 1980): 25.

9 DEVELOPING THE CIRCULATION MANUAL AND STAFF TRAINING PROGRAM

A major portion of the implementation project will consist of the project manager and project team compiling an institution-specific circulation manual and planning a program for staff training on the new automated circulation system. These two tasks are closely related, since the circulation manual will play a significant role in training library staff on how to use the new automated circulation system.

THE CIRCULATION MANUAL

The circulation manual should document circulation policies and procedures that will be implemented once the new automated circulation system is activated. All circulation policies and procedures should be included in the manual, whether or not they are directly related to functions that will be performed using the new automated circulation system. Policies should be described in full, and step-by-step instructions should be detailed for each procedure. Use non-technical language that can be understood by all staff members—from the most to the least experienced—since, in addition to documenting policy and procedural decisions, the circulation manual will serve as a handy source of reference for staff overwhelmed by the many details that must be learned in order to operate the new system. By using the circulation manual in conjunction with the vendor-supplied system documentation, staff will have at their fingertips information about how system functions operate, as well as information about how the new automated circulation system will be used in their particular library.

FORMATTING THE CIRCULATION MANUAL
The circulation manual may consist of one volume detailing both policies and procedures for circulation activities *or* it can be separated into two volumes—one for policies and one for procedures.

A manual that consists of one well-organized, indexed volume is easier to use, since it eliminates the need to decide whether the policy volume or the procedure volume will be consulted. If the one-volume format is selected for the manual, each entry should: 1) briefly explain the system function; 2) describe situations in which the function should be used; 3) detail, step-by-step, how the function should be used; and 4) include or cross-reference any policies that govern the use of the feature (see Fig. 9-1). A two-volume manual should include the same information divided between the two volumes.

The body of the manual should include a title page, a table of contents, the actual policies and procedures, and an index. The entries in the manual may be organized in a number of ways. Two of the more useful arrangements are an alphabetical arrangement of the specific headings that describe individual entries (i.e., charge, discharge, manually-created patron records, tapeloaded patron records, recalls, etc.), or broader headings that group entries together by common concepts (i.e., item records, patron records, borrowing privileges, etc.). To make the manual even simpler to use, sections may be tabbed with brief descriptors.

To accommodate the fluid dynamics of policy and procedure formation and revision (and to ensure that the manual can be kept as current and accurate as possible at the lowest cost possible), a loose-leaf notebook is recommended as the most easily-updated format. If each page includes the manual title, the section descriptor, the date of the page's origination/revision, and the page number to two decimal places, revisions will be easily accommodated. For example, "Circulation Procedures Manual" and "October, 1993" could be placed on two lines at the bottom left of the page, and "Charge/Discharge" and "p. 3.51" could be placed on two lines at the bottom right of the page (see Fig. 9-1).

DISTRIBUTING THE CIRCULATION MANUAL

If possible, the manual should be ready for distribution prior to beginning staff training on the new automated circulation system. This makes the trainers' task easier, since the manual can be used both as an instructional tool during the training process and as a handy reference manual after training has been completed. During the training sessions, the circulation manual should be referred to frequently so that staff have ample time to acquaint themselves with its organization and contents. Whether or not the circulation manual is used as part of the formal staff training program, copies should be distributed prior to the activation of the system to

---

FIGURE 9-1 Sample Pages from a Circulation Manual

Charge/Discharge: Non-Circulating Items

The Circulation system tables are defined in such a way as to allow library staff to charge to pseudo patrons "Lost" and "Missing" items that normally do not circulate. The table configurations will also allow these non-circulating items to be charged to real patrons, if an exception has been approved according to your unit's policy (check with your supervisor for further information on your unit's policies).

To charge a non-circulating item to "Lost" or "Missing," follow the normal charging process using the appropriate pseudo patron records (see page 3.00 of this manual for a full description of the charging process; see page 14.00 for more information about pseudo patron records).

A. TO CHARGE NON-CIRCULATING ITEMS to patrons other than "Lost" or "Missing," follow these steps:

    1. Modify the item record.

        — *Retrieve* the item record by typing "f it =," followed by a scan of the item's barcode.
        — Tab to the NOTE field and enter a *note* indicating that the temporary location must be removed and the loan code changed back to the original loan code of [state the original loan code] when the item is discharged.
        — Tab to the TEMP LOCATN field, select a location code that includes circulating items and enter this code as a *temporary location*.
        — Tab to the LOAN CODE field and key in the *new loan code* by typing "plcy."
        — Set the *flag* that will alert Circulation staff, on the item's discharge, to review this item; to do this, tab to the REVIEW field and type "x" in front of "Circulation."
        — *Press "enter"* until "Done" appears at the top of the screen, indicating that the item record has been modified.

    2. Charge the item to the patron using the standard charging procedure.

CIRCULATION PROCEDURES MANUAL   **CHARGE/DISCHARGE**
October, 1991   p. **3.51**

FIGURE 9-1   (continued)

B. TO DISCHARGE NON-CIRCULATING ITEMS that have been charged to patrons other than "Lost" or "Missing," follow these steps:

1. On discharging the item, the *review flag* message will appear stating that the item needs to be reviewed by circulation staff; follow your unit's policy for handling items that need review.
2. To review the item, *retrieve the item record* by typing "f it" and scanning the barcode; read the message in the note field.
3. Remove the *temporary location* by tabbing to the TEMP LOCATN field and pressing the EOF key.
4. Tab to the LOAN CODE field and type the *original loan code* over "plcy."
5. Remove the *circulation flag* by tabbing to "Circulation" in the REVIEW and pressing the EOF key.
6. Remove the *note* by tabbing to the NOTE field and pressing the EOF key.
7. *Press "enter"* until "Done" appears at the top of the screen, indicating that the record has been modified.

all library units in which the new automated circulation system will be utilized.

When determining how many manuals to print and distribute, bear in mind that each manual distributed will also need updating as policies and procedures are revised, added, or eliminated. To save staff time and economize on costs associated with the updating process, it is possible to limit the number of manuals that will be distributed. The project manager, project team, and managers of the circulation units should each receive their own copy of the manual. If used in training sessions, one manual for each training workstation is also necessary. Beyond these requirements, manuals can be distributed to workstations or service desks, rather than to individuals, and shared among staff who work in these areas. Depending on how many workstations are in a unit, how heavily-used they are, and how closely they are grouped together, one or two manuals in an area should suffice.

REVISING THE CIRCULATION MANUAL

Although the project manager and project team may be responsible for the initial development of the policy and procedure manual, develop some mechanism for future updating of the manual. Whenever policies or procedures are changed, or new ones added as gaps are detected, add new or revised documentation to the manual. This keeps it as current and accurate as possible and guarantees its usefulness as a source of reference. Shortly after the system is activated, when policies and procedures are tested by real situations in the workplace, misconceptions, gaps, and errors will emerge at an alarming pace. This is a natural consequence of having developed policies and procedures prior to the system becoming operational for daily use. As long as a procedure has been devised for updating the documentation and this procedure is promptly activated, a great deal of fine-tuning can take place in a short period of time.

After this initial flurry of revisions, the need to update portions of the manual will continue to surface regularly for any number of reasons. Responsibility for this task may be assigned to a group of individuals—preferably a representative group of individuals drawn from library units where activities will be effected by changes in circulation policies or procedures. This group could be a subset of individuals drawn from a larger advisory group, such as a group of circulation staff who routinely meet and advise library administration on circulation issues. Updating procedures should detail who is responsible for drafting text for the manual, duplicating and distributing the revisions, what support staff will be available for typing, and how revisions will be approved and by whom.

THE STAFF TRAINING PROGRAM

It is essential that library staff have some notion of how to operate the new automated circulation system prior to its implementation. Staff who are provided non-threatening, unpressured learning opportunities prior to using the system on a day-to-day basis will find adjustment to the new system less painful and will be well-prepared to cope with the system once it is operational. This, in turn, will help promote staff acceptance of the new automated circulation system, and, ultimately, will be a major factor in determining the success of the system. Participation in task-oriented groups during the course of the implementation project will acquaint staff with various aspects of the new system. The information acquired through this type of involvement will, however, provide an incomplete, fragmented view of the new system and its functions. A comprehensive training program that is delivered systematically to library staff is the best means for providing a well-rounded view of the system. Unless use of the system will be limited to one or two individuals, a formal training program is the most efficient way of achieving an economy of scale in instructing the many staff who will be using the system. A formal training program also ensures that consistent information about the new automated circulation system is conveyed to all staff members.

Ideally, the training program should target *all* library staff, although it will not be necessary for all staff to acquire the same level of detailed knowledge about the system. For instance, a member of the reference staff might only need a general overview of how the new automated circulation system will work and how to interpret circulation system messages on the OPAC. In contrast, staff at circulation service desks will need detailed instruction on the operation of all system functions.

There are an infinite number of ways to approach staff training, with the format and content of the training program depending greatly on the size and needs of the staff in any particular library. However, the development of any staff training program will need to take into consideration the following questions:

1. What information is required by each staff member? Can these requirements be merged into instructional components aimed at groups rather than individuals (e.g., circulation staff, fines staff, reserve staff, technical services staff, library administration, etc.)?
2. What format or combination of formats will provide the most effective and efficient means for delivering information about the new automated circulation system to a staff with diverse information needs (e.g., formal classroom presentations, self-paced individual instruction using print or computer-based exercises, one-on-one tutoring, etc.)?
3. Who will develop the details of the program? Who will be responsible for delivering any training that is not self-instruction?
4. Where and when will the training take place? Are there areas within the library that are relatively isolated and can be used for uninterrupted instruction and practice on the system?

Prior to developing the details of the staff training program, consider asking the vendor of the new automated circulation system to provide training for the individuals who will be developing and delivering the staff training program—in essence, a program to train the trainers. Most vendors will, for a fee, provide on-site training. Once these key individuals have been trained, they can train the rest of the library staff. They can accomplish this by using the program and materials provided by the vendor or by developing an individualized program that is tailored to the specific needs of the library staff within that particular library.

CONTENTS OF THE TRAINING SESSIONS

Since the new automated circulation system will be used by many individuals in a variety of library units, a training program that addresses the diverse needs of these staff members will consist of a number of components, perhaps utilizing different instructional techniques and formats.

1. An Introduction or Refresher Course on System Basics

If the new automated circulation system is part of an integrated system that includes other previously-installed modules, an introductory or refresher course may be needed to orient staff to the equipment and basic commands that are used to operate the automated system. Staff in circulation units may have had little reason before now to use other modules within the automated system, and system navigation techniques that other library staff have grown accustomed to using may be new territory for circulation staff. Without a basic understanding of keyboard configurations and system commands, the multitude of functions and commands that must be used in the circulation system will confuse and overwhelm trainees. To avoid this, an introductory or refresher component should precede any instruction on specific functions in the circulation module. Staff should be allowed to familiarize themselves with the terminal keyboards in their work areas, and with common system commands ("forward," "back," "clear," "reset," etc.). For staff who have been trained previously on system basics but have not used their knowledge much or at all since training, it may be that some simple handouts or self-paced exercises are all that is needed. On the other hand, staff who have never had any training or occasion to use the automated system will need in-depth instruction, through one-on-one tutoring or formal classroom training sessions.

If the library does not have the resources for on-going system training, there may be staff in other library units who will see an introductory or refresher course on system basics as an attractive training opportunity, whether or not their job will require them to use the automated circulation system. Though intended as part of the automated circulation system training program, staff interest in these sessions may be broader. If the library staff is fairly large, and resources don't allow for general system training for all library staff in the course of this particular training program, it may be necessary to limit trainees in these sessions to only those staff whose jobs will require them to use the circulation system.

2. Training for System Hardware and Software Operation

If the computer that runs the automated circulation system will be operated by library staff rather than by staff within the agency, institution or organization's computer center, individuals responsible for overall system operation will need to be trained on both the hardware and software that will run the system. Training needs in this area may be minimal if other modules of an integrated system have already been installed. In that case, all that may be needed is training on the jobs that must be run and maintenance that must be done as part of the circulation module. Training for these individuals should be provided by the vendor of the system.

3. General Orientation to the Automated Circulation System

After the introductory or refresher course on system basics has been completed, training for the automated circulation system may begin with a general orientation to the automated circulation system. This general overview of the system should be offered to all library staff, whether or not they will actually use the system as part of their daily duties. Any presentation should keep in mind that the audience will consist of a wide variety of staff groups, from administrators who will never touch a keyboard but need to know how the system works and what benefits it offers, to circulation desk attendants who will need to know in great detail how the system will be used for their daily tasks.

A review of the structure of the automated circulation system (and its relation to the rest of the automated system if the circulation system is one of many modules within an integrated system), the databases that will be used in the circulation system, and the functions that will comprise the circulation system will suit most staff members' information needs. It is also useful in the general overview to provide some context for the system, e.g., how different functions will be used in various library units, and what general impact the system will have on the way staff currently perform their required tasks. For those staff members who need minimal information about the automated circulation system, this general session should provide enough information to satisfy their curiosity and enable them to answer questions from outside the library, yet avoid inundating them with extraneous information. A demonstration of key features in the automated circulation system may be of interest to participants in a general orientation session, but hands-on training of all participants is not necessary.

The general overview will be the only system instruction many staff members will need to receive. For those who will go on to more in-depth, hands-on training on specific system functions, the general overview should provide a larger perspective in which to place the system specifics that will follow in subsequent training sessions.

4. In-Depth Training on Circulation System Functions

The in-depth training that follows the general orientation to the system is best offered through a format that requires each trainee to interact, hands-on, with the system. A hands-on approach improves trainees' retention of the material by allowing them to experience first-hand what happens when everything goes smoothly as well as what happens when errors occur. Generally, the most manageable approach to in-depth training on the automated circulation system is to divide the information about the system into logical units or sessions, each one focusing on a specific system function or series of related system functions. For an example of how a comprehensive staff training program might be constructed (see Fig. 9-2).

All in-depth training sessions should include instruction on how to perform the various functions on the circulation system, as well as any applicable data entry guidelines or policies or procedures that affect or are affected by each system function. Role playing or the presentation of detailed, real-life scenarios during the training sessions will help present system instruction in the context of the workplace and actual situations trainees are likely to encounter once the system is operational.

To ensure consistent information delivery for multiple sessions within each training module, particularly desirable if a number of individuals will be assisting as trainers, scripts may be developed which detail the contents and presentation sequence of each training module (see Fig. 9-3). It is not necessary for the trainers to read, verbatim, the contents of the script when they are delivering training sessions. This, of course, would be a dull and ineffective way to deliver the information. However, trainers should follow as closely as possible the sequence in which concepts are introduced and the amount of detail presented. Extemporaneous tangents during training sessions will be unavoidable, but should be kept to a minimum to avoid confusing trainees with too much information. Scripts for the training sessions can be developed by the individuals who will take part as trainers. The project manager and project team also will need to be involved in this process if they are not participating as trainers.

Scripts will be fine-tuned after many drafts have been developed and tested, and after much agonizing has been done by the individuals developing the training program. As planning progresses, "dress rehearsal" training sessions can be arranged, culling "trainees" from staff who are unfamiliar with the new automated circulation system. These dress rehearsals help identify weak, unclear or erroneous information, and point out shortcomings in the organization or presentation of the sessions. In addition to helping identify problems with session content, rehearsals also help any trainers not accustomed to public speaking achieve a higher comfort level for speaking in front of a group.

Each script should incorporate ample time for trainees to ask

---

FIGURE 9-2 A Sample Program for Comprehensive Staff Training on the New Automated Circulation System

MODULE #1: **SYSTEM FUNDAMENTALS**

Description: Two hour, hands-on session

Audience: Staff who will be required to use the new circulation system and who need to learn or re-learn the basics of keyboarding and system search commands

Content: Keyboarding; system commands; records in the system and retrieving them

MODULE #2: **CIRCULATION SYSTEM OVERVIEW**

Description: One hour presentation (no hands-on)

Audience: All library staff

Content: Basic concepts surrounding item, patron, bill and fine records and how they relate to the circulation system; charge, discharge, renew, recall, billing, back-up functions in the system; staff and public system messages; samples of notices, bills, statistics produced by the system

MODULE #3: **ITEM RECORDS**

Description: Three hour, hands-on session

Audience: All staff who will be using the circulation system

Content: Relationship between bibliographic and item records; fields in item records; retrieving item records; creation, modification, deletion of item records; difference between linked (permanent) and unlinked (temporary) item records; withdrawing lost or discarded items

MODULE #4: **PATRON RECORDS**

Description: Three hour, hands-on session

Audience: All staff who will be using the circulation system

Content: Fields in patron records; sources for patron records; retrieving patron records; creation, modification, deletion of patron records; charge lists for individual patrons; "pseudo" patron records for library units or functions; proxy records

MODULE #5: **CHARGE/DISCHARGE/RENEW/RECALL**

Description: Three hour, hands-on session

Audience: All staff who will be using the circulation system

Content: Charging, renewing, discharging items; placing, cancelling, resequencing recalls, rush recalls, holds; handling blocked patron or item records; placing staff review flags; "courtesy" features (e.g., charging, discharging, renewing, recalling at units other than the item's "home" unit)

MODULE #6: **BILL AND FINE**

Description: Two hours, hands-on session

Audience: All staff who will be interpreting or negotiating fines in the circulation system

Content: Information included in bill and fine records; automatically and manually creating bills; how financial blocks are created and how to handle them; posting payment to individual records; adjusting fines and crediting accounts

---

FIGURE 9-3   Staff Training Script

The following is a portion of a script developed for staff training on the charge function.

CHARGING

Now we get down to the business of charging materials. You've begun the process in some of your earlier training sessions, and some of you may feel you know it all already. Please be patient and stay with the group; it will make the session easier for all of us. This includes *not* keying in anything at your terminals until I give you explicit instructions to do so.

**TRANSPARENCY 6:   TWO WAYS TO CHARGE

Let me summarize the two ways to get a charge screen before we actually try it on the terminals.
   1.   You can clear the screen; type the transaction code (lcum), a space, and the charge command (char), and press enter;
   2.   Or, you can clear the screen and simply press the PF7 key.

Now let's all try the first method:
   Clear your screen.
   Type **lcum char** (don't forget the space) and press the **enter** key.
This is what you should see:

**TRANSPARENCY 7:   CHARGE SCREEN

Now let's try the second method:
   Clear your screen.
   Press the **PF7** key.
The charge screen consists of the following [point out on the transparency]:
*the transaction code LCUM
*the DONE command
*the current date and time
*the name of the screen display, "charge or renew item"
*the identification code of your terminal session (this will be important to note since with LUMINA Circulation you will be using more than one session on your terminal, each dedicated to a different purpose)
*the patron ID field (your cursor is automatically positioned in this field, but can be moved around by using the tab key).

FIGURE 9-3 (continued)

At the very bottom of your screen you will see prompts [point to them on the transparency]. These prompts will tell you what options you have for the next step. They appear on all the screens that you will be using and they are in both the production and training modes.

For the next step in charging, find the patron ID marked "A" on your exercise sheet.

Your cursor should be positioned in the patron ID field.

Scan the patron barcode (you do not have to press the enter key after scanning a barcode; this is automatically supplied by the scanner).

**TRANSPARENCY 8: CHARGE SCREEN WITH PATRON ID AND PROMPT FOR ITEM ID

Notice what has happened. The patron ID now appears on the screen along with the patron category and patron name [point to each on the transparency].

Further down on the screen, the cursor has been automatically positioned in the same ID field.

Note that the bottom of the screen includes prompts for charging an item or for starting over if something is wrong with the patron ID.

Now we have to supply the item barcode. Find item 1A on your exercise sheet.

Scan the barcode.

What you should see is the following:

**TRANSPARENCY 9: SUCCESSFUL CHARGE

You get a message that the charge has been successful and a due date. If there will be a receipt printer attached to your terminal in your work unit, a due date slip would be produced at this point for you to give to the patron.

**TRANSPARENCY 10: DUE DATE SLIP

Due date slips will look like this and include the following information [point out on the transparency]:

*the date and time of the charge

*the item barcode number

*the patron barcode number

*the due date

*the item call number

*a brief bibliographic description of the item.

questions. One effective way to do this is to have actual prompts written into the script. At the conclusion of each sub-topic within a script, the trainer should be prompted to ask if the trainees have any questions. And, of course, trainers should have time to answer questions that arise at other, non-prompted times as well.

At the conclusion of each training session, participants should be encouraged (and immediately given some time if possible) to practice the concepts they have learned. Take-home exercises, or more structured "lab" sessions scheduled to follow each training session, could supplement the formal, hands-on training sessions. At a minimum, the trainees should leave with the trainers' names and phone numbers in hand in case questions or problems arise once they begin to practice system functions on their own.

TRAINING NEEDS OF DIFFERENT STAFF GROUPS

The training program model presented in the previous section, a model based on sequential components that progress from an overview of the system to a detailed explanation of the system's finer points, allows library staff to select which training sessions to attend based on the information they will need to fulfill their job responsibilities. By staff groups, these training needs might be as follow:

1. Library Director, Administrators and Managers; Administrative, Clerical, Reference, and Collection Development Staff.

A general orientation to the new automated circulation system will fulfill the information needs these staff groups will have. They should acquire a basic understanding of the system so they are able to promote the system and answer questions about it among interested groups or individuals outside the library.

2. Managers of Units that will use the new Automated Circulation System.

Managers of units where staff will be using the circulation system should receive in-depth training on all system functions staff in their units will be using. This not only fosters a firm understanding of how the automated circulation system will be used in their units, but also enables the manager to troubleshoot system problems and provide capable guidance and hands-on assistance in emergencies. If the circulation system will be implemented as another module in an integrated automated system, the refresher course reviewing system commands may also be included as part of these individuals' training. Whether or not this additional training is needed will depend on the level of experience individual managers have had with the automated system prior to the implementation of the circulation module.

3. Full-time Staff in Circulation, Course Reserves, Technical Services, Document Delivery, Fee-Based Services, or Interlibrary Loan Units.

These staff groups will probably be the most active users of the new automated circulation system. In order to effectively and efficiently perform their many circulation-related tasks on the system, these groups will require a particularly intensive training regimen. They should receive a general orientation to the system followed by in-depth, hands-on training on all circulation system functions. Pairing the overview with in-depth training will promote a broad understanding of the system as well as detailed knowledge of the array of functions the system will perform.

4. Student Assistants, Volunteers or Part-Time Staff in Circulation, Course Reserves, Technical Services, Document Delivery, Fee-Based Services, and Interlibrary Loan.

These staff groups will be the second most active users of the automated system, however, their information needs are likely to be more narrowly defined than those of the staff groups listed in the third category. To accommodate these special needs, staff members falling into these groups should receive a general orientation to the system, followed by in-depth training on those functions they will be likely to use in their jobs rather than all the functions the system will offer.

The above guidelines will help determine how many staff will need a general orientation to the system versus the number who will require in-depth, hands-on system training, and will assist in finalizing the number of training sessions to be offered. Guidelines are only guidelines, however, and there will be exceptions for staff whose responsibilities overlap work areas, or for staff who are simply curious about the new system. Although it is critical that staff who will actually be using the system have hands-on training, it is not essential for those who are merely curious about the system. Training sessions may be structured so one or two curious "observers" may sit with and watch trainees who are assigned to the terminals for hands-on training.

TRAINING FORMATS

Training can be as formal or informal, as structured or unstructured, as the developers of the training program see fit. The format selected will depend on a number of factors, including the number of staff who must be trained prior to the implementation of the system, the period of time in which the training program must be completed, and the number and type of training facilities available.

Training formats include formal sessions presented in a classroom setting, workshops, seminars, self-paced instruction or computer-assisted instruction, and one-on-one tutoring. It is not necessary for each component in the training program to be presented in the same format. The format may even vary by staff group. For instance, full-time circulation staff may receive in-depth training on system functions in a formal classroom setting, whereas student assistants in circulation units may be trained individually on selected system functions by a full-time staff member in the work unit. The least economical approach in terms of staff time is one-on-one tutoring. Depending on whether or not training "scripts" are used for these one-on-one sessions, this method may also present more opportunities for inconsistent information delivery among trainees. However, a one-on-one approach does allow the trainer to focus her/his entire attention on one individual, delivering the information in a way that makes sense to that particular individual and making sure each concept is understood. Self-paced instruction may not be flexible or sophisticated enough to answer questions the trainee may have as he/she proceeds with the program. This is less of a drawback with computer-assisted instruction. With a hypertext software program, possible questions from trainees can be anticipated and answers included in the program. However, it is not always possible to anticipate every question a trainee might have, and the development of such a program is costly in terms of staff time. One of the more practical, economical approaches is training that takes place in a formally-structured classroom setting where many staff are trained simultaneously, information delivery is consistent and questions may be answered as they arise. The major drawback to this format is its inflexibility in adapting to different learning styles and paces.

Whatever instructional format is selected, it is essential that the in-depth training sessions include ample opportunity for trainees to experience hands-on interaction with the system. As mentioned earlier, hands-on experience with the system is a very effective technique for reinforcing concepts presented in a training session. Ideally, the in-depth hands-on training should take place after all the system hardware has been received and installed. However, if the equipment has been delayed and the implementation date for the system is rapidly approaching, it is better to train staff on whatever equipment is available prior to implementation, rather than wait until the equipment arrives and system is about to become operational, leaving staff unprepared to operate the system.

Hands-on practice is usually relegated to a training region that mirrors the production region in every way except, perhaps, size. Setting aside a special training region and encouraging staff to practice what they've learned in training sessions allows individuals to experiment with the system in a "safe" setting (e.g., no library users are waiting, and no errors will negatively impact the production region).

TRAINING SPACE AND EQUIPMENT

Ideally, the library should set aside some space apart from any work unit in which training can take place. This will vary depending on the training formats selected by the library. It may be as simple as a single work station in a quiet corner of each library unit, or as complex as a classroom that will be shared by all library staff and which includes multiple workstations and a variety of instructional media (overhead projectors, videocassette players and monitors, overhead terminal displays, etc.). By setting aside a space for training, the trainees are removed from the distractions of their work areas and can concentrate fully on learning the new system. The hardware configuration for each training workstation in the designated training area(s) should match as closely as possible the hardware configuration that staff will encounter in their work units. This allows the trainees to adjust to the mechanics of the equipment, familiarize themselves with the placement of characters on the keyboard, and practice positioning the barcode readers to successfully scan barcodes.

TRAINING MATERIALS

Training materials will include those used in the training sessions by the trainers and trainees, and those that are intended for use as supplemental references after training has been completed. Materials can be distributed in advance of scheduled training sessions so that staff have time to study them and formulate questions, or they can be distributed at the training sessions. Relying on trainees to review training materials prior to the training session is risky business. Finding time to accomplish this is often difficult. Even if trainees do find time and are motivated to review the materials, they may not understand them until after they have completed the training. In addition, if materials are distributed prior to the training sessions, trainees will need to remember to bring their packets to the training sessions. For these reasons, distributing materials during the training sessions is preferred. If, however, materials will be distributed prior to the training sessions, maintain a ready stock of extra packets at the training site(s) for forgetful trainees.

Whatever distribution method is selected, the following materials will be needed during classroom training sessions:

1. For the Trainees . . .

    a. Vendor-supplied documentation, including system manuals.

    b. Library-supplied documentation, including the circulation manual.

    c. Workbooks or xeroxed copies of exercises and test records from the patron and bibliographic databases that will be used during the session.

    d. Handouts summarizing important points covered during the training session.

    e. Glossary of unfamiliar terms to which trainees will be introduced in the training session.

2. For the Trainers . . .

    a. A copy of all the training materials that will be given to trainees.

    b. Any equipment supplemental to the hardware required for the training workstations, such as an overhead projector with spare bulbs, blank transparencies, and marking pens; a television monitor and videocassette player; a portable liquid crystal display for projecting online interaction with the system; extension cords; etc.

    c. Easel with paper pad and markers; masking tape or pins.

    d. Pointer or light pen.

    e. Session script and any supplemental graphics such as overhead transparencies, posters, graphs, charts, videotapes, etc.

At the conclusion of the training session, the trainers should send the trainees back to their work units with the following items:

Practice Exercises: The first exercises trainees should be asked to complete are those that allow each trainee to create a series of patron and item records for their own use in subsequent practice exercises. It should be clearly conveyed during training sessions that practicing with records currently existing in the training database is forbidden, since those records have been set up specifically for training sessions. (See Fig. 9-4 for an example of practice exercises.)

Ready Reference Handouts: These handouts should provide abbreviated lists of key system commands and functions covered during the training sessions. (See Fig. 9-5 for an example of a ready reference handout.)

System Documentation; Circulation Policies/Procedures: If they are not used in the training sessions or being distributed by any other means, copies of vendor-supplied and/or library-supplied documentation that are to be used in work areas should be provided to some (if the documentation will be shared) or all (if each individual will have their own copy) trainees.

List of Contacts: A list of the names, electronic mail addresses, and telephone numbers of trainers or other resource people who can be contacted with questions should be provided for each trainee. Trainees should be encouraged to contact these individuals with any questions that may arise after training has been completed.

AFTER TRAINING

Immediately after the formal training program has been completed, trainers may want to reinforce certain concepts by testing or quizzing staff on system functions. This is a technique that is often applied to new student assistants. It frequently goes beyond testing knowledge of system functions only, by including an assessment of the individual's knowledge of circulation policies and procedures. A second follow-up approach does not involve testing the trainees, but rather observing them, in either a systematic or random fashion, as they interact with the system once it is operational.

Testing or observing staff after training is a helpful starting point for identifying and clarifying misconceptions about the system, as well as identifying what follow-up training is needed. Follow-up training to reinforce the initial training can be provided if the library has the staff available to provide this supplemental training, and time to complete it before the system is actually operational. Supplemental, follow-up training allows staff to approach the system in a more knowledgeable fashion than during the initial training, and provides them with another opportunity to ask questions that have arisen since their initial exposure to the system. Supplemental

FIGURE 9-4 Staff Training Practice Exercises

SESSION III:
CHARGE/DISCHARGE/RECALL/HOLD

Exercises

1. **Charging/Discharging/"Browsing" an Item**

   a. **Charging an Item**

      Press [PF7] to get a charge screen.

      Scan the barcode on Sally's ID.

      Scan item #1's barcode.

      Charge three additional items to Sally by scanning the barcodes for items #2, #3, and #4 while on the same charge screen.

      Clear your screen.

   b. **Charging an Item Already Charged to Another Patron**

      Press [PF7] to get a charge screen.

      Scan the barcode on Joe's ID.

      Scan item #1's barcode (just charged to Sally).

      When the message "not charged--currently charged to another patron..." appears, you may either type "n" to stop the charge process, or "y" to continue.

      To continue, simply type "y" and press [Enter]. The system will simultaneously discharge the item from the patron in 1.a., and charge it to the patron in exercise 1.b.

      Clear your screen.

FIGURE 9-4 **(continued)**

Charge/Discharge

      c.   **Discharging an Item**

         Press PF8 to get a discharge screen.

         Scan item #1's barcode (just discharged from Joe).

         Clear your screen.

      d.   **"Browsing" an Item**

         Press PF8 .

         Scan item #5's barcode. The message, "not discharged--item was not charged" will appear.

         Clear your screen.

         Type "LTUL fi it=" and scan the item barcode to retrieve the item record. Note that a "browse" has been recorded in the BROWSE field.

  2.   **Placing Recalls, Holds, Rush Recalls**

      a.   **Placing a Recall**

         Type "LTUL reca=" and scan the barcode on Joe's ID.

         Type "fi it=" and scan the barcode for item #2, currently charged to Sally.

         Type "sele" over "done" or "more" and press Enter . You are now at the recall/hold screen.

         Type "r" in the "request type" field.

         Press Enter . The message, "recall and hold(s) placed" will appear.

         Clear your screen.

         Following the preceding steps to place an additional recall on item #2 for Peter.

         Do not clear your screen.

FIGURE 9-5   Sample Ready Reference Handout

▼ **Patron Record: Summary**

Transaction Code: LPTF   Law: LPLF

To display patron record

    • by patron name: LP_ _ find pn=_____

    • by patron ID (barcode) number: LP_ _ find pp=_____

    • by patron record number: LP_ _ patr _____

    • by patron organization ID number: LP_ _ find po=XX_____
       (where XX is the Patron Group code
       of the file where record was created)

To display list of items charged out to patron (HAS list)

    • all items: LP_ _ has   <patron id/barcode>

    • only recalled items: LP_ _ has reca <patron id/barcode>

    • only overdue items: LP_ _ has over <patron id/barcode>

To create patron record   LP_ _ cpat

To add a new address
    1. Display patron record.
    2. Request new address section using CREATE NEW (x) ADDRESS field at the
       top of the patron record.

To change the status of patron ID to "stolen" or "lost"
    1. Display patron record.
    2. Change ID STATUS field to **STOL** or **LOST**.
    3. Add appropriate note codes to NOTE field.

---

12   *LUMINA Circulation Training Manual*

training also allows trainees to focus more clearly on those concepts that may have perplexed them during the initial training. Yet another benefit to follow-up training is that it allows the trainers to identify problem areas or gaps in expertise and correct them.

Staff training on the automated circulation system does not end once the system becomes operational. Enhancements or changes to the system software, newly-hired staff, or staff who were not required previously to use the system, all will require that training beyond the initial program be provided. These situations underscore the need to make system training an on-going responsibility of the library. Ideally, the library should have on staff an individual responsible for on-going, library-wide system training. Unfortunately, many libraries are not willing or able to devote a staff position to this task. If no staff member is assigned responsibility for systems training, alternatives should be considered, such as bringing in vendors or other systems specialists to provide training for system enhancements or changes, or sending selected staff members to programs and workshops provided elsewhere with the understanding that they will train other staff on their return.

A FINAL WORD OR TWO ABOUT THE STAFF TRAINING PROGRAM

A staff training program is an essential part of the over-arching implementation plan for the automated circulation system. Staff will learn more in training sessions than simply how to operate the new system. Instructing staff in the functions of the new automated circulation system, including how and when those functions will be used, allows trainees "to gain better insight into their jobs," and, as a consequence, allows them to become more effective in their daily roles.[1] A program must be developed, trainers identified, training facilities set up and scheduled, training scripts written, handouts and manuals prepared, a schedule of training sessions publicized and the attendance of session participants coordinated, and test records created to support the training activities. With the infinite array of large and small tasks associated with a staff training program, it is never too early to begin the planning and preparation process.

Also, once the switch is thrown and the system is operational, no matter how thoroughly and consistently staff have been trained, there will be some individuals who will be more timid than others in their use of the system. The project manager, project team, and trainers will be called on often in the first months of operation to do a fair amount of hand-holding with certain staff members. This will mean less time is available to perform the infinite trouble-shooting and fine-tuning that the system's implementation will generate. However, time spent supporting staff as they adjust to the new system should be considered time well-spent and a normal part of the implementation process. Taking time to gently lead wary staff members toward more confidence and independence with system operation will yield long-term benefits in promoting staff acceptance of the new system.

REFERENCES

1. John Corbin, *Managing the Library Automation Project* (Phoenix, AZ: Oryx Press, 1985): 158.

10 FACILITATING STAFF ADJUSTMENT TO THE NEW SYSTEM

It is worth remembering that the success or failure of a computer-based system is usually due to the people involved, much more than to the characteristics of a particular system. It is possible to give numerous examples of terrible systems which work because the staff are supportive, and good systems that do not work very well at all because the staff are opposed.[1]

The advent of a new automated circulation system is bound to generate conflicting emotions within staff members who will be using the new system. In addition to their excitement about the new system, and their hope that it will reduce or eliminate formerly tedious tasks and improve service to library users, staff will also experience some trepidation about the new system, especially if this is the first automated circulation system for the library. Any new experience automatically dictates some degree of change, but the uncertainty of what changes will be brought about by installing a new automated circulation system can undermine enthusiasm and support for the new system if the planning and implementation project is mishandled.

A REVIEW OF APPROACHES

One way to make the psychological transition easier for staff, is to implement the new system in stages. Various ways to phase in an automated circulation system will be discussed in Chapter 12. Another way to make the transition easier is to make sure that as many library staff members as possible, particularly those whose jobs will be directly affected by the new system, play some role in the planning and implementation process. Some degree of participation will help staff develop a familiarity with the system that supplements any training received, and will help allay fears as the unknown becomes more of a known entity. Furthermore, the more staff who participate in the implementation planning process (whether they are assigned tasks to complete or simply serve as consultants to the project manager and project team), the less likely it is that issues or tasks important to system implementation will be overlooked. If two heads are better than one, a multitude may be better yet in identifying and correcting oversights in the implementation process before any damage is done.

In addition to formal or informal staff participation in implementation project tasks and discussions, staff anxiety about the new system can be diminished by: a) a comprehensive staff training program, b) clear, complete in-house documentation in the form of a circulation manual, and c) a list of individuals who may be contacted with questions about the new system. During the training program, many questions staff may have about the new system will be answered, and the number of unknown variables associated with the system will decrease as staff acquire knowledge about the system. The circulation manual will supplement the training program by providing staff with a ready source of reference that can be consulted whenever questions arise. Staff members' comfort level in operating the new system will be raised, knowing they have at hand a convenient resource that will fill in gaps left in their memory after their training has concluded. A list of individuals who are willing to serve as system "experts" also provides a valuable information resource (as well as a comfortable safety net) for staff. A more detailed discussion of these two areas can be found in Chapter 9.

Highlighted in this chapter are two more elements that are important in facilitating staff adjustment to the changes the new automated circulation system will bring. These are: 1) a broad communication effort that will highlight information about the new system and provide regular reports detailing the progress of the implementation project; and 2) a strong network of user support that will be available to staff during the implementation process as well as after the system is operational. A staff-directed public relations effort and support network together with staff involvement in the implementation project, a comprehensive staff training program, a well-conceived circulation manual, and a list of system experts who may be consulted with questions will all help to decrease staff members' anxieties about the new automated circulation system and to increase their sense of ownership of the system. This in turn will lead to greater staff acceptance of the new system and increase the odds for a successful implementation of the system.

PROMOTING THE SYSTEM TO LIBRARY STAFF

Although the library will be doing its best to involve as many staff as possible in the implementation project, it is not likely that staff will be aware of every aspect of the new automated circulation system or of the project to implement it. A large portion of the public relations effort promoting the new automated circulation system will be directed toward library users (see Chapter 11); however, it is important to include library staff as well when developing a comprehensive public relations strategy to support the implementation of the new system. Communicating information that may be useful or of interest to a specific, targeted audience is the basis of any public relations effort. The type of information that will be of use or interest to library staff will include:

1. regular updates summarizing the progress of the implementation project,
2. highlights of specific system features, and
3. announcements of policy and procedural changes that will be in effect once the new system is operational.

As pointed out earlier, regularly communicating information in these areas to library staff can be an effective means for allaying staff fears and securing their acceptance of the new system. To that end, any communications to library staff should incorporate a good measure of sensitivity as to what thoughts and feelings staff might be experiencing about the new system and the changes it will bring.[2]

STAFF AUDIENCES TO TARGET

Although it is important that all staff be targeted as part of the public relations effort, there will be groups within the library staff who will have different information needs and to whom specific communications should be addressed.

Staff in circulation units will be most interested in details about system functions and policies and procedures that will accompany the implementation of the system. Information that will provide clues as to how their daily tasks will be changed once the system is operational will be welcome by these staff members. The goal of communications directed toward circulation staff should be to remove as much mystery as possible about the system and its possible impact before the system becomes operational. Information should be presented in the context of whatever is relevant to the jobs these staff members perform. Another appreciative audience of this type of information will be staff in units where the new automated circulation system will be used. Staff in technical services, course reserves, document delivery, and interlibrary loan units will also want to know how the new system will impact their daily tasks.

Two other staff groups who will have special information needs are the library managers and administrators. These individuals must be kept apprised of the project's process in more detail than any other portion of the staff. They will also require a concise overview of system functions and capabilities. Library managers' and administrators' responsibilities include varying degrees of liaison work with individuals and groups outside the library. Managers and administrators supplement externally-directed public relations efforts and must be able to accurately and knowledgeably represent the new automated circulation system.

Library managers and administrators each have additional information needs that differentiate them from each other. Managers who are responsible for units where the new automated circulation system will be used will need advance notice of system details that will be important to staff and operations in the areas for which they bear responsibility. Knowing these details in advance of training (which often does not occur until the end of the implementation project) will assist managers in planning for the changes that will occur in their units as a result of system implementation. In addition to reports on the general progress of the implementation project, library administrators also need to be kept informed about the problems that inevitably arise during the course of an automation project, including projected pitfalls, bottlenecks, or negative staff reactions to the system.[3] Keeping administrators informed of these situations provides the project manager and project team with valuable allies who have more options at their disposal for remedying some of these problems.

SYSTEM FEATURES TO HIGHLIGHT

A good automated circulation system will sell itself, reducing the effort needed to convince library staff that the system is indeed a good one.[4] If the system is a sound one, it will provide many benefits for both library staff and users. Highlight those benefits, taking care not to promise job improvements or functions that the system cannot deliver. Although it is difficult to accurately predict how every detail of the new system will function once it is in operation, general concepts can be identified during the implementation process and promoted to the library staff. For instance, automating the charge process may not eliminate queues at busy service desks, but it will eliminate the need to manually fill out charge cards, thus reducing the time it currently takes to charge an item to a library user.

Public relations communications for library staff should emphasize how the new automated circulation system will make it easier for staff to do their jobs well and serve library users more efficiently. This information will vary with the targeted audience. For instance, technical services staff may be more interested in how the system will simplify record-keeping for items sent to the bindery, whereas circulation desk staff may be more interested in how the efficiencies of the charge function will reduce library user complaints at service desks. For all staff who will be using the new circulation system, emphasize which tedious tasks will be eliminated thereby allowing them to devote more time and effort toward other more interesting areas. For public services staff, emphasize the positive impact the system will have on library users and how a happier clientele will improve the interpersonal interaction staff will experience with users.

PROMOTIONAL TECHNIQUES

Some vehicles for effectively promoting the new system to library staff and keeping them informed about the progress of the implementation project can include the following:

1. The Library Newsletter, General Mailings, Electronic Mail

The newsletter, mass mailings, and electronic mail can be used interchangeably (depending on the communication networks established within the library) to achieve wide distribution of information about the system or the progress of the implementation project. Use these to distribute any documentation (including plans, timelines, meeting minutes, drafted policies, procedures or forms) that pertain to the project. In addition, these resources can be used to distribute short feature articles about the system and regular reports of the progress of the implementation project.

2. System Demonstrations

A series of system demonstrations can be presented by individuals most actively involved in the implementation project, e.g., the project manager, members of the project team, system trainers, etc. In addition to a general demonstration of the variety of functions the system can perform, additional sessions focusing on a few key functions that will be of interest to specific staff groups are generally very well received.

3. Field Trips

Field trips or visits to other libraries where the system has already been implemented allow staff to see the system operating in a real-life setting. It also provides staff with an opportunity to talk with colleagues who are currently using the system.

4. Verbal Reports

Announcements and verbal updates can be delivered by the project manager or project team members at general meetings of library staff or meetings of selected committees or staff groups. An additional bonus to this form of communication is the opportunity the audience has to ask questions of the presenter, or to request more detail about specific points covered in the presentation.

AFTER IMPLEMENTATION

Public relations efforts pertaining to the new automated circulation system will diminish in intensity after the system is operational; however, this communication process will continue in varying degrees throughout the life of the system. Efforts will be needed to communicate to library staff: 1) any system or operational landmarks, including progress being made in converting manual circulation records; 2) explanations for any system problems or malfunctions; 3) enhancements made to the system, including fixes, new releases, etc., and 4) any changes in policies or procedures that have library-wide ramifications.

ESTABLISHING A NETWORK OF USER SUPPORT

Prior to the implementation of the automated circulation system, the project manager should coordinate a network of user support external to the library. Contacts within this network will offer support supplementary to that provided by the system vendor, and will play a key role in staff acceptance of and comfort with the system. This network should provide a variety of supportive contacts, all of them useful at different times to meet different needs.

CONTACTS AND VISITS TO OTHER LIBRARIES

Other libraries where the new automated circulation system is currently being used can serve as gold mines of information, during the implementation project as well as after the system is operational. By talking to experienced colleagues at these libraries, staff in libraries beginning to implement the same system can find out what to expect with the new system and reduce or eliminate the possibility of unpleasant surprises. Colleagues in libraries where the system is currently operational can alert newcomers to situations that won't be covered in the vendor's documentation, such as how the library's procedures can be expected to change, and what techniques are effective for coping with system shortcomings. Tapping into this valuable experience can save the library much time and energy in the implementation process and eliminate the need to reinvent the wheel previously invented in another library. It is also encouraging to discover firsthand just how creative library staff can be in adapting an automated circulation system to the needs of a particular library.

Try to include a few site visits to other libraries where the system is currently in use. Observing the system in use can be enormously helpful, eliminating some of the guesswork as to how the system will perform in the actual workplace. Site visits are also excellent opportunities for talking to the host library's staff. Inquiries can be made about what problems were encountered during system implementation, and how staff training was conducted. In addition, requests can be made for samples of printed materials that were generated during the host library's implementation project, including handouts, quick reference guides, training scripts, and in-house documentation or manuals.

In addition to the information that can be collected, a site visit also establishes one or more contacts at another library using the same automated circulation system. These individuals (with their permission, of course) can be contacted with questions throughout the course of the implementation project and beyond, as long as both institutions are still using the same automated circulation system.

SYSTEM-SPECIFIC USER GROUPS

Recognizing the importance of support among users of a common system, vendors have begun organizing system-specific user groups for most major automated library systems. These user groups can be local, regional or national, and, if the system is an integrated system, often are subdivided further into module-specific groups, such as circulation, acquisitions, OPAC, etc. Many meet at regional or national conferences and include vendor representatives among each group's participants. User group meetings serve as a forum in which system updates and enhancements may be announced, questions about common user problems may be addressed to vendor representatives, and advice may be asked of other libraries. Some of the more active user groups can also serve as catalysts for system changes and enhancements.

LISTSERVS

Another useful forum for asking advice of other libraries, and for sharing information discovered by trial and error, is a vendor-specific listserv or electronic bulletin board. If the library is experiencing a specific problem, asking for other libraries' solutions via electronic mail is a very effective way to receive input very quickly from a number of sources. Individuals are not competing for the limited time at a user group meeting, and anyone may respond to a question. At least one response to a specific query is bound to directly address or can be adapted to address the problem presented in the original question.

To find out which automated system vendors offer listservs for their customers, contact the vendor of the automated circulation system the library has purchased, or consult a directory that lists these electronic resources.[5]

REFERENCES

1. Joseph R. Matthews and Kevin Hegarty, *Automated Circulation: An Examination of Choices* (Chicago, IL: American Library Association, 1984): 122.
2. Michael J. Bruer, "The Public Relations Component of Circulation System Implementation," *Journal of Library Automation* 12 (September 1979): 216.
3. Bonnie Juergens, "Staff Training Aspects of Circulation System Implementation," *Journal of Library Automation* 12 (September 1979): 205.
4. Bruer, "The Public Relations Component of Circulation System Implementation," p. 217.
5. Addresses for electronic network resources are available in *Directory of Electronic Journals, Newsletters, and Academic Discussion Lists,* Fourth Edition (Washington, D.C.: Association of Research Libraries, Office of Scientific and Academic Publishing, 1994); Edward T. L. Hardie and Vivian Neou, *Internet: Mailing Lists* (Menlo Park, CA: SRI International, 1992); and, Donnalyn Frey, *!•@: A Directory of Electronic Mail Addressing and Networks* (Sebastopol, CA: O'Reilly & Associates, 1990).

◥◣◥◣ WORKING WITH LIBRARY USERS

Once the new automated circulation system is operational, library users will quickly discover the benefits of such a system, particularly if the library's previous circulation system was manual. First to be noticed, no doubt, will be the improved service at circulation service desks as routine transactions are completed quickly and efficiently, and queues for service are reduced. Library users will also appreciate the ready availability of accurate circulation information for specific items in the library collection. And, as library staff settle into new routines and grow accustomed to working with the system, library users may find themselves the recipients of new services that the library was unable to offer in an environment of manual record-keeping. Clearly, library users will become primary beneficiaries of the new automated circulation system.

Just as library staff will need to be kept informed about the changes that will occur as a result of the implementation of the new automated circulation system, so will library users. Even though the changes on the whole will be positive, change is change and library users must be prepared. In addition to alerting library users to forthcoming changes, communicating with this group prior to the implementation of the new system provides the project manager and members of the project team with an opportunity to short-circuit any misconceptions (from idealizations to negative views) that may arise in an environment where the system and its impact remain a mystery. A public relations program that includes extensive publicity and a training program (if any system functions will be self-service) will play an important role in preparing library users for the arrival of the automated circulation system.

PUBLICITY

In a nutshell, the program to publicize the new automated circulation system to library users can be summarized as follows:

> Tell 'em what you're going to do, do it, and tell 'em what you've done.[1]

The public relations program should begin as early as possible, whenever the library begins receiving concrete information about the new system. The first communication distributed under the auspices of this program should be an announcement of the purchase of the system (including very general information about what the new system will offer library users) and a projected target date for system implementation. As the implementation date moves closer, communications should become more frequent, include more detail, and employ a wider variety of media to distribute the information. The objective is to introduce library users to the system before it becomes a day-to-day reality, rather than to try to sell the system after it has been implemented.[2]

IDENTIFYING THE AUDIENCE

Part of developing a well-thought-out public relations program is the identification of the audience or audiences the publicity is intended to reach. For instance in academic libraries, the primary audience will be the campus population (e.g., faculty, staff, and students). The staff group may include an added dimension, (e.g., staff in campus offices who interact with the library as part of job responsibilities such as staff in the bursar's, student records, or identification card offices) and have very different information needs than individuals who use the library for personal reading or research. In addition, publicity might also be directed to external, off-campus users if they comprise a large segment of the user population. External library users may include private citizens, network participants, reciprocal affiliates, or coordinate campus users in larger universities. Different approaches can be devised for each group, since each will have different interests and concerns. Faculty may be more interested in how the renewal process works for long-term loans, students might be more interested in how the system's efficiencies will streamline the charge out process at service desks, and external users may be most interested in how they go about obtaining borrowing privileges under the new system. In public libraries, the primary audience will be the residents of the community in which the library is located, ranging from children to adults, and including current users and non-users of the library. Businesses or companies who use the library's services or materials may also be targeted. School libraries will want to include both students and teachers in their target audience, and corporate libraries will focus public relations efforts toward employees of the library's parent company. Whatever the target audience, both users and non-users of the library of the library should be included if possible, since each non-user has the potential to become a library user.

WHAT INFORMATION SHOULD BE COMMUNICATED?

What types of information should be conveyed in a well-constructed public relations program directed at current and potential library users? First, it is important to set a positive tone by pointing out the benefits that library users will experience with the implementation of the new system. Even though the mechanics of operating a good automated circulation system should be transparent to all but library staff, library users won't be able to avoid noticing differences in the way the library conducts its business after the system has been implemented. These differences should be emphasized, and their positive attributes highlighted. How will the new automated circulation system save library users time, or improve their access to information about the availability of library items? If the charge out process will be quicker and more efficient, say so. If self-service will be an option for charging or renewing materials or for requesting items be recalled or held, announce this service enhancement with a description of how quick and easy this will be. If circulation records will be more accurate and circulation information about specific library items available for the first time via public access terminals, this should be pointed out. If the efficiency of the discharging process on the new system means that library materials will be reshelved more quickly, highlight this important improvement.

When pointing out improvements that will result from the implementation of the new system, it is very important that these improvements be described in realistic terms. Improved existing services and the development of new user services will be of great interest to the user community. However, don't make promises that cannot be kept. For instance, don't announce that materials will be re-shelved moments after they're discharged on the system, unless it can actually be done as consistent practice. All communications should be upbeat, yet realistic. This will be true whether the communication is a printed announcement that will be read by many individuals, or a spontaneous discussion that occurs between a library staff member and library user at a service desk. An enthusiastic attitude on the part of the library staff, tempered with honesty about the system, will encourage strong support for the system. In addition, the information provided in these communications should be limited to facts about the system, and not include speculations about its potential capabilities. This approach will save the library many embarrassing moments explaining why the system can't do what was promised in a brochure or newspaper article. Raising service expectations to levels higher than what can actually be met runs the risk that anything short of these expectations will be perceived as a failure by library users.

Second, the library needs to point out any changes that will affect the way in which library users have routinely used library services or collections. This should include any modifications to library policies or procedures that will directly impact library users. If, for the first time in recent history, library users will be required to produce library cards when charging materials, they need to be informed of this change prior to their first visit to the library after the system has been implemented. In addition, library users will need to be told how to go about registering for and procuring a card that will allow them to charge library materials. Changes in how due dates will be calculated (e.g., moving from a fixed due date to a rolling due date), loan policies (changes in loan periods for specific patron categories or specific library materials), fines rates (especially increasing rates or imposing fines in areas where previously none were used), and any sanctions for delinquent library users should all be clearly communicated so there are no unpleasant surprises once the system is operational.

In addition, any attendant activities necessary for the implementation of the automated circulation system, such as retrospective conversion of bibliographic records and barcoding of individual library items, should be announced. An explanation of what the project will entail, any disruption it will generate, and how it will assist with the implementation of the new automated circulation system should be conveyed. In particular, retrospective conversion and barcoding projects are massive undertakings that will result in major accomplishments. Care should be taken to conduct well-planned projects, inform the user community what these projects will mean to the library and the new system, and advertise the progress of the projects. Celebrating their completion with special events that include library users can help underscore the magnitude of accomplishment realized by the completion of these projects. These projects can serve as landmarks along the way to the implementation of the new automated circulation system, each building more excitement and anticipation for the final implementation.

Third, the library should provide some target date or dates when the system will be implemented, and the aforementioned benefits and changes realized. Remember, however, that delays occur and timelines and target dates can be expected to change. Any target dates or timelines for public consumption should take this into consideration and be appropriately broad given the proximity of the system's actual implementation. For instance, "1995" might be the target date announced at the very beginning of the project, replaced by "Fall 1995" as the project progresses and a more precise date can be estimated with greater accuracy. In addition, a contact in the library (preferably the implementation project manager) should be identified as a resource for further information.

Any detailed information communicated about the system or its capabilities should be presented at a level appropriate for the audience targeted by the communication. Do not be tempted to save time by using the same communications for both library staff and library users. If communications within the staff public relations program have followed the guidelines presented in Chapter 10, they will be framed in a context that is not meaningful to library users, and will contain a level of technical detail that is unnecessary for their needs. In libraries such as public or school libraries where both adults and children comprise the target audience, communicating at the appropriate level may require at least two approaches, possibly more.

As a general rule of thumb, any communications directed toward library users should avoid too many technical details about the system. Information overload in this area may confuse, bore or alienate the intended audience. Keep the information short, simple and accurate.

PROMOTIONAL TECHNIQUES

The formats and media employed to convey messages about the new automated circulation system should vary. A single communication or promotional technique is not sufficient given the variety of questions that will need to be answered and, in some libraries, the diverse audience that will need to be reached. Below are some of the possibilities the library may want to explore when developing its public relations program. Some approaches will work better than others with different audiences and in different situations. Generally, they will fall within one of two groups: 1) those techniques appropriate for use onsite (e.g., within the library itself), and 2) those techniques that are more appropriate for use offsite (e.g., outside of the library building).

1. Onsite Promotional Techniques

Promotional techniques used within the library building generally fall into two categories: 1) those that stay within the physical confines of the library, and 2) those that are distributed in the library but which library users can take away with them.

Displays and posters placed in strategic locations in the library, particularly near service desks that will utilize the new automated circulation system or near public access terminals that will provide information from the new system, are an effective way to reach library users. As library users interact in the very areas that will be affected by the new system, information about the system is presented in a context that is immediately relevant, allowing them to compare the present situation with that anticipated for the future.

System demonstrations are also an effective way to reach library users. Library staff can offer demonstrations on demand or at preannounced times; or, a terminal or simulated program may be made available for library users to explore the new system on their own. System demonstrations may be particularly effective if the library plans on including in the new system any self-service component for library users. Even something as simple as placing as-yet-nonfunctional computer terminals in public areas prior to the system becoming operational will generate interest in the coming system.

Brochures, pencils with printed messages, handouts, bookmarks, flyers, leaflets, and single-page announcements are all effective ways to provide library users with information they can take with them when they leave the library. The printed communications may be made available in a rack of handouts or on a display table, or circulation staff may tuck them into individual items as they are charged at service desks.

A barcoding project that uses volunteers from the user community is a good way to introduce library users to the new automated circulation system as well as to previously undiscovered portions of the library collection. Offering training sessions for self-service charging in libraries where this will be a service option and announcing the need for library users to register for borrowing cards also will advertise the new automated circulation system.

2. Offsite Promotional Techniques

Free publicity is always available from news media looking for an interesting story. Don't wait for local newsletters or newspapers to discover the breaking story. They may not "discover" it until the new automated circulation system is up and running. Take the initiative and contact reporters with your story. By taking the initiative with the media, the project manager or whomever is making the contact is given the opportunity to emphasize the elements of the story they choose. It also allows the story to be placed within a positive context, highlighting improvements that will result from the implementation of the system. Waiting, for instance, for the student newspaper to initiate contact could result in the story being told by a cub reporter who thinks the most interesting way to present the new system is in a negative context (e.g., overdues, fines, unhappiness with loan periods, etc). The key is to make the initial contact before such a situation develops and to present the story in the most interesting terms possible, perhaps capitalizing on a unique element of the automated circulation system or the implementation process. For instance, discuss how unique the retrospective conversion process was in comparison to that undertaken in other similar libraries (the largest, the most comprehensive, etc.). Construct a creative press release or stage an event that dramatizes the benefits of the new system. A catchy headline or opening sentence in a press release is critical in capturing attention, as is a symbolically staged event highlighting a key accomplishment of the project (for instance, a dramatic disposal of the manual records that are no longer needed). Ask the local newspaper to send someone to photograph the first charge on the new system. Also helpful when interacting with reporters, especially during interviews, is a "fact sheet" listing the most interesting features of the system. A fact sheet can dramatically reduce factual errors in the final stories and can alleviate the tedium of answering common questions about the system.

Publications within the larger agency, institution or organization of which the library may be part (departmental newsletters, the student or campus newspaper, newsletters sent to students' parents, etc.), and school or campus radio stations offer an excellent opportunity to reach both users and non-users of the library. Local newspapers, radio and television stations are especially useful media resources for public libraries, but may also be worth exploring by other types of libraries if they serve a large group of library users outside the parent institution or organization. Larger academic or public libraries who participate in regional or national shared resources programs may want to send announcements to regional or national library and academic publications.

Electronic methods of communication should also be included if available or appropriate. Announcements via electronic mail and subject-oriented bulletin boards, discussion groups, or listservs will reach a variety of potentially interested individuals. Electronic media is quick and avoids printing and duplicating costs.

Meetings with groups, such as library advisory groups or boards, offer an excellent opportunity to promote the new system and answer any questions those in attendance may have. One danger is that sessions such as these may turn into gripe sessions about the library that have nothing to do with the new automated circulation system, or with circulation activities at all (e.g., "The copies from the library photocopiers are terrible. Can't they be improved?"). In the case of issues that are totally unrelated to circulation, the best approach is for the library representative to admit that he or she is neither prepared nor qualified to deal with these extraneous issues and suggest the group contact the library director or another appropriate staff member if they are interested in further pursuing these issues. Issues that pertain to circulation, but are not directly related to the system (e.g., "Why can't unbound periodicals circulate?"), should be dealt with if the library representative is knowledgeable about the issue, but care should be taken that this does not divert the discussion into areas that were not intended. Every attempt should be made to re-direct the discussion back to the issue at hand, the new automated circulation system. For instance, a question about why it takes library staff so long to re-shelve library materials can be answered in the current context, segueing into an explanation of how the new automated system should help relieve this situation.

Direct mailing of the more polished, informative pieces that may also serve as give-aways within the library, such as a professionally printed brochure describing the system and the enhancements and changes it will bring, are also useful if allowed by the library budget. This format is one of the few that can be structured broadly enough to meet a variety of library users' information needs. This is an important advantage since it probably will not be economically feasible to develop, print, and distribute a series of brochures, each with a different emphasis targeted for a different group within the targeted audience. One "all-purpose" brochure can be devised containing general information about the system. Avoid the temptation to provide too much detail and include only those concepts that will be of common interest to all or the majority of the library's users (see Fig. 11-1).

AFTER IMPLEMENTATION

One of the most important yet often overlooked elements to any public relations program is its on-going nature. Public relations, whether for library staff or library users, does not come to a crash-

FIGURE 11-1   A Sample Brochure Describing the New Automated Circulation System

YET TO COME . . .

Software is being developed to support the automation of course reserve. Once reserve activities are automated, the charging process will become as streamlined as it is for materials circulating from the general, non-reserve collections. In addition, you will no longer need to visit your reserve unit to determine what readings have been set aside for a course. Course reserve lists will be accessible from any LUMINA terminal.

CIRCULATION IS BEING AUTOMATED

Beginning in Fall 1991, the University of Minnesota Libraries will offer greatly improved service when all circulation units switch from manual to automated circulation on LUMINA, the University Libraries' automated system.

This latest enhancement of LUMINA will allow library staff to charge, renew, and recall library materials more quickly and efficiently for library users.

The University of Minnesota is an Equal Opportunity Educator and Employer.

FIGURE 11-1 (continued)

CHECKING OUT MATERIALS

Barcoded ID Card Needed

As of Fall 1991, you will need your new barcoded ID card to check out library materials. Students without this new barcoded ID should contact the ID Office, 248 Williamson Hall (625-9357). In most cases, you will no longer need to present a fee statement as items are checked out — LUMINA will handle that detail.

Current Mailing Address

LUMINA will also handle another bothersome detail; you will no longer need to fill out charge cards. LUMINA will automatically match your records to whatever address you have given the University as your current address.

Recall notices, overdues and other library-related mail will be sent to that address. Please be sure that the University has your current local mailing address if it is different from your permanent home address. Address change forms are available at Williamson Hall or at any circulation unit.

Loan Periods

BOOKS:

Undergraduates, Special Privilege Card
holders, Alumni, Extension, etc.:   6 weeks

Graduates, Faculty, Staff: 13 weeks

PERIODICALS:

Periodical loan periods may vary at different libraries. Ask circulation staff for more information.

Another bonus with LUMINA is that due dates will be calculated from the charge date. This means you will always have the same number of days to use your items, no matter what time of the quarter you borrow them. This also means that individual items checked out on different dates will also be due on different dates. Be sure to note the date due, listed on the date due slip provided with each item.

RENEWING MATERIALS

Item Barcode and Patron Barcode Needed

You will need to provide a barcode number, found on the back cover of most library materials, for each item you'd like to renew. In addition, your patron barcode, listed on your ID card, must also be listed. Make sure you provide complete information each time you renew an item — renewal requests submitted with incomplete information may be subject to fines.

Renewal Limits

Books charged to non-faculty patrons may be renewed a total of two times. If a book is still needed after two renewals, it must be brought to the library and charged out again. Periodicals may be renewed three times before they must be brought to the library.

RETURNING MATERIALS

Returning library materials will be easier than ever, as you will be able to return most of them at any of the University Libraries. Our new automated system allows us to record your returns at any library. Reserve items and periodicals, however, still need to be returned directly to the library from which they were borrowed.

ing halt on the day the new system becomes operational. After the system has been implemented, the public relations program for library users will broaden and become the responsibility of all library staff using the system. Staff at service desks will need to take immediate remedial action whenever a library user has a bad experience with the system. Prompt action on the part of library staff will reduce considerably the possibility of the situation getting out of hand and short-circuit the formation of any negative perceptions about the system or library staff's capabilities.

Library staff who interact with library users at service desks will also be able to identify any common misperceptions library users have about the new system. For instance, if a large enough number of library users appear to think barcodes are part of the library's security system (and are removing them from the books in an attempt to thwart the security system), this may be addressed by posting throughout the book stacks copies of a short announcement explaining how barcodes are used, supplemented by a short article in the campus newspaper.

In addition, any time there is any further change, such as a system, policy or procedural change that impacts library users, the particulars will need to be communicated to library users as soon as possible. After the implementation project has concluded, responsibility for these communications can be shifted from the project manager to the circulation advisory group.

TRAINING FOR LIBRARY USERS

As more self-service features appear in the automated library system marketplace, more libraries are experimenting with allowing library users to charge, renew or recall library materials. At least two companies are now marketing self-service workstations that simultaneously charge and desensitize library materials for library users. If the library targets items as part of its security system, a workstation that simultaneously charges and desensitizes items is the most practical way to implement self-service charging. Otherwise, library staff will still be needed to desensitize materials after library users have charged them, undermining the concept of self-service. Staff would need to double-check each item's record to make sure that item has been charged properly to the patron before desensitizing the item, creating a process more time-consuming than simply maintaining enough service desk staff to charge library materials for library users.

If any self-service features will be offered to library users after the new automated circulation system is operational, consideration will need to be given to whether or not a training program will be offered to library users. Most self-service workstations are designed to be simple to use and are extremely user friendly, requiring little if any training of library users (see Fig. 11-2). The online prompts at the self-service workstation may suffice for user instruction, or may be supplemented with additional printed handouts or quick reference guides. If user training is deemed desirable, it may be offered as a stand-alone training or orientation session or incorporated into broader user instruction or orientation sessions.

ESTABLISHING LIAISONS OUTSIDE THE LIBRARY

Depending on how the library plans to enter patron records into the circulation system, how the data in patron records will be used, and who is responsible for running the system software, establishing regular communication via a liaison or liaisons to the following non-library offices will help address system problems effectively and efficiently.

IDENTIFICATION CARD OFFICE
If the library is going to require library users to produce an identification card from the library's parent institution or organization when borrowing library materials, establishing regular communication with staff in the office that produces the identification cards (and whatever database may support this activity) is essential. Problems will arise with alarming frequency over expired or incorrect identification cards. Having a contact in the identification card office will help library staff resolve these problems as quickly as possible. In addition, if the library imports its patron records from the database that produces identification cards, records that miss a tapeload or provide incorrect information for individual patron records will need to be corrected in both the library's and the identification card office's databases to ensure that future tapeloads include the correct information for these records. Establishing a

FIGURE 11-2   A Sample of Online Instructions in a Self-Service Charging/Desensitizing system

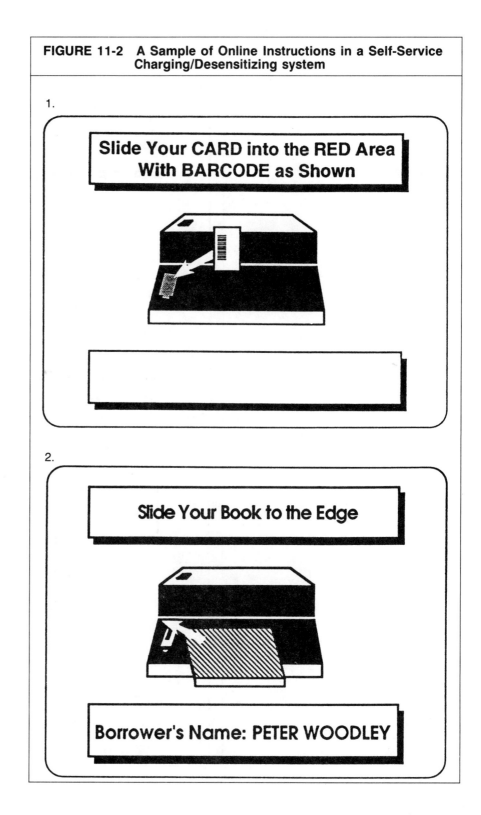

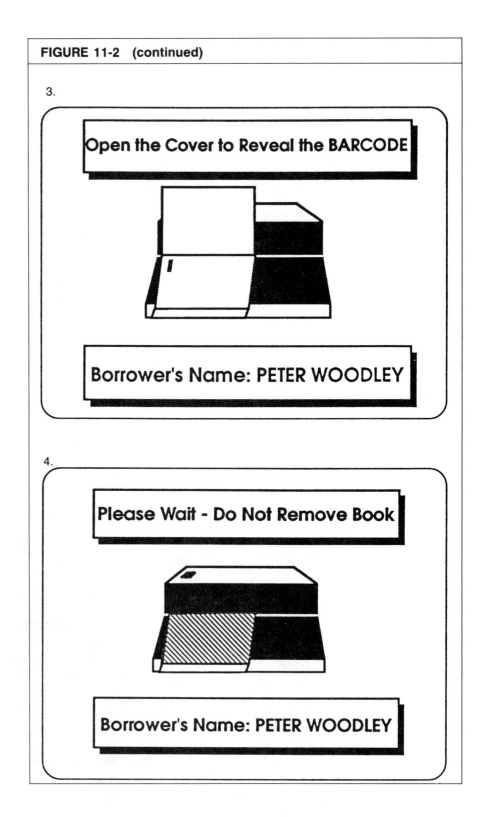

FIGURE 11-2 (continued)

3.

Open the Cover to Reveal the BARCODE

Borrower's Name: PETER WOODLEY

4.

Please Wait - Do Not Remove Book

Borrower's Name: PETER WOODLEY

FIGURE 11-2   (continued)

5.

6.

liaison with this office will also allow both parties to achieve a greater understanding of how and why errors occur and what quick fixes and more permanent measure can be taken to correct errors so that library service is unimpeded. Regular contact between library staff and staff in the identification office and the teamwork this interaction encourages will also help reduce or eliminate finger-pointing when things do go wrong.

HUMAN RESOURCES/PERSONNEL OFFICE

If the library will be importing an employee database from the Human Resources or Personnel Office of the parent agency, institution or organization, regular contact between staff in this office and library staff will be needed for the same reasons as those detailed above for the Identification Card Office.

BURSAR'S OFFICE

In academic libraries, electronic links between the library and the Bursar's Office are not uncommon. These links allow the library to electronically transfer data about outstanding fines and fees individual students have incurred to records in the Bursar's Office's databases. This eliminates the paperwork and time delays that can accompany written requests for holds to be placed on delinquent students' records or registration. If the library will be establishing this type of link, a liaison will need to be appointed to work with the Bursar's Office, trouble-shooting the system when necessary and developing policies and procedures for this activity.

MISCELLANEOUS OFFICES OR DEPARTMENTS

If the library has decided to create a patron database by importing data from non-library databases, there may be large groups of library users who will not have records in the imported databases. In an academic library this might include alumni, summer-only students, evening students, or students who take classes but are not enrolled in a degree program. Establishing liaisons with offices or departments representing the interests of these library users is an excellent way of promoting positive public relations with these groups. In addition, if these offices or departments have their own in-house databases with information that could be useful for creating patron records, it may be possible to work with staff in these offices to import the data into the library database.

Even if the library has installed and is running its own computer for the automated circulation system, it still will be useful to establish some sort of communication (formal or informal) between the library's systems staff and the parent agency, institution or organization's systems staff. In addition to providing a conduit for sharing information about technical innovations, brainstorming troubleshooting solutions with other non-library systems experts can provide a fresh perspective.

REFERENCES

1. Michael J. Bruer, "The Public Relations Component of Circulation System Implementation," *Journal of Library Automation* 12 (September 1979): 218.
2. Joseph R. Matthews and Kevin Hegarty, *Automated Circulation: An Examination of Choices* (Chicago, IL: American Library Association, 1984): 120.

12 SYSTEM START-UP

As the start-up date for the new automated circulation system gets closer, three more issues will require the attention of the project manager and project team. First, how will the new system actually become operational? What approach will be taken to "throw the switch?" Second, when and how frequently will the various batch programs that support the operation of the new system be run? And third, will the statistical reports that will be supplied by the new system be adequate or will additional statistical software programs be needed?

THROWING THE SWITCH

The ultimate goal of the implementation project is to finally turn on the new automated circulation system for everyday use. Reaching this goal does not necessarily mean the project is at an end. Some tasks, such as the evaluation of the system, cannot be completed until after the system has been in use for a certain length of time. However, reaching the point at which the switch is thrown and the new system is ready for use does mean the major objective of the project has been realized. There are four basic approaches that can be employed to make the new system operational within the library. Although presented below as discrete approaches, many libraries will use some combination of the four rather than rely solely on one approach.

1. The Pilot Project Approach

Prior to implementing a new automated circulation system library-wide, one of the best ways to extensively test it is to conduct a pilot project in one of the smaller, self-contained service units within the library or library system, such as a multi-function service desk or a branch library. Conducting a pilot project presents an excellent opportunity for testing and debugging the system hardware and software before the system is implemented on a large scale. It also allows staff to test the procedures and policies that have been developed to support the new system and to correct or fine-tune them as needed. Debugging and fine-tuning the system will occur whether or not a pilot project is conducted, but a pilot project can make this an easier process by allowing problem resolution on a smaller scale with minimum disruption. Once the bugs have been eliminated and the system is operating smoothly in the test unit, implementation of the system throughout the rest of the library or library system may proceed with a diminished potential for disaster.

When selecting a service unit in which the pilot project is to take place, consider the following variables in order to conduct the best test possible. First, the service unit selected for the pilot project should be, for the most part, a self-contained unit that handles all the work that will be affected by the new automated circulation system, including:

1. performing all basic circulation activities such as charge, discharge, recalls, holds, etc.,
2. processing and maintaining records for course reserves activity if a reserve module will be part of the new automated circulation system,
3. calculating and processing bills and fines for its library users, and
4. performing technical service tasks related to its collection.

A branch library often embodies this relative independence, and would be an appropriate site for the pilot project. Another possibility might be a subject collection that is housed in a building with other library units but is treated as an independent library.

Second, when selecting a site for the pilot project, consider the volume of circulation activity. To adequately test all system functions, policies, and procedures, the volume of circulation activity should be high enough that a variety of activities and situations will be encountered during the test period, but low enough that troubleshooting problems will not cause major service difficulties. The many problems that are inevitable during a pilot project should not create major inconveniences or result in dramatically slower or poor service for library users.

Third, the staff in the unit selected for the pilot project should be willing, even eager, participants. Ideally, the staff in the pilot project unit will consist of flexible, mature individuals who will be constructive in their approach to the testing process. If possible, avoid staff who are likely to respond negatively or hysterically each time a new problem is encountered. Staff involved in the pilot project will be closely watched by staff in other units where the new system will be implemented. A positive attitude on the part of staff involved in the pilot project will lay the groundwork for a successful implementation of the system on a larger scale. As staff in other units witness the successful implementation of the system in the unit conducting the pilot project, their level of anxiety about the new system will be reduced.[1] The larger-scale implementation following the successful pilot project will generate less stress, and staff in subsequent units will be inspired to repeat the success of the pilot project unit.

2. The Module-by-Module Approach

Depending on the software the library has purchased for the new automated circulation system, some modules of the system may be in a more imperfect state of development, potentially presenting more problems than solutions if implemented. For instance, the system could consist of a very sophisticated module that provides functions for basic circulation activities (charge, discharge, renew, recall, etc.), an imperfect but acceptable module that provides functions for calculating and processing bills and fines, but only a primitive, unsatisfactory module for processing and maintaining records for course reserves. Since the system modules for basic circulation and bill and fine are inextricably interdependent, the decision might be made to bring up both these modules simultaneously, even if the bill and fine functions aren't entirely acceptable. However, the implementation of the course reserves module could be postponed until the other two modules were fully implemented and staff accustomed to their operation. Delaying the implementation of this last, perhaps less critical module also may buy more time until the vendor is able to provide a substantially-improved course reserves module in a new release of the system software. However, the software for automated circulation systems varies, as do the needs of the libraries purchasing these systems, and this parceling of system software into independent modules may not be possible.

3. The Side-by-Side Approach

The most conservative and costly approach for implementing the new automated circulation system is to run both the old and new system side-by-side for a period of time. This may be the best approach if the consequences of the system's failure or a botched implementation would be substantial.[2] This approach allows testing of the new system while using the safety net provided by the old system. If major problems are encountered on the new system, the old system is available as an immediate substitute until the problems are resolved. Obviously, the expense and staff time involved in duplicating all circulation transactions are considerable. In addition, the weaning process can drag on as staff become more and more reluctant to disengage from the old system. This reluctance can intensify after staff discover that the new system is neither perfect nor the panacea for all their circulation woes. Under these circumstances, it is possible that staff will convince themselves that the old system was better and refuse to accept the new system.

One way to effectively utilize the side-by-side approach is to develop a timeline for phasing out the old system. The time it will take to convert circulation records from the old system to the new, the period of time over which attrition will significantly reduce circulation records in the old system, and the time it will take to test all the new system functions, policies, and procedures, can all be useful in determining the timeline for phasing out the old system. A predetermined date for phasing out the old system also forces staff to accept immediately the fact that reliance on the old system will not be allowed to continue for an indeterminate length of time. Having a goal in mind is helpful in psychologically preparing library staff to accept the system within that time period.

4. The "All-for-One and One-for-All" Approach

If the library is relatively small, consisting of only one or two circulation service points, it is possible to implement the new automated circulation system all at once throughout the library, simultaneously abandoning the old system. If this approach is used in a larger system, however, extensive planning and coordination will need to proceed the actual implementation. Both the hardware and software will need to be rigorously tested prior to the system becoming operational. In addition, any conversion of records into the machine-readable format required by the new system must be completed prior to the date when the new system will become the sole source of circulation information. This approach is the most stressful for library staff and holds, potentially, the most pitfalls for larger library systems. Although this approach will probably work quite well for a library with only one or two circulation service units, or even for the larger library system converting from one automated circulation system to another, it is not the most effective way for a large, complex library system to implement its first automated circulation system.

SELECTING AN APPROACH TO MAKE THE NEW SYSTEM OPERATIONAL

Any of the above approaches, or any combination of them, will prove successful in different libraries for different reasons. When deciding how to bring the system into full operation, answering the following questions will help determine what approach or mix of approaches is likely to be most successful:

1. In what degree of readiness is the equipment that will support the new system? Is all electrical and telecommunications wiring complete? Has all of the equipment been installed and tested so it is ready to function?
2. Is the library small or large? Is it a simple or complex organization? How many different library units will be coming up on the new system?
3. How prepared are library staff to begin using the new system? Have they completed training? Are they eager and willing to begin using the system?
4. What would the consequences be, for both library staff and users, of an unsuccessful attempt to make the new system operational?

OPERATIONS SCHEDULES

Although online systems can be differentiated from batch-processing systems by their ability to conduct transactions in "real" time versus the batch processing method of holding transactions and processing them at a previously-scheduled time, most online systems will have a component of batch-processing for operations that can be postponed until there is computer time to complete them. Batch programs in an online circulation system may include such things as printing daily operation reports, statistical reports, patron notices, and the like. They may also include programs to regenerate indexes to incorporate any changes that have been made in database records since the indexes were last regenerated (such as indexes for patron records, bibliographic records, or bill and fine records), and to delete any records that have been withdrawn from the databases. These batch programs need to be scheduled to run on a regular basis. If the automated circulation system has been installed on a computer within the library, the library staff will determine when batch programs will be scheduled to run on the computer. If the automated circulation system has been installed on a computer in the central computer center for the agency, institution or organization, library staff will need to consult with the computer center staff to determine the scheduling of the circulation batch programs on this shared computer. In addition to scheduling the times and days for these programs to be run, a staff member (library or computer center staff, depending on where the computer is housed) must be identified to initiate the batch processes, mount any magnetic tapes of data that the programs will use, and monitor the system as it processes the programs (e.g., handling error reports, loading paper into the printer, etc).[3]

If the automated circulation system will be part of a previously-installed integrated system, the scheduling of the circulation batch programs must be balanced with the scheduling of batch programs supporting other applications in the system (e.g., acquisitions, serials, the OPAC, etc.). The needs of other applications in the system, and the needs of the library staff and users, must be weighed and balanced with other demands on the computer running the system and the costs associated with computer time and the paper generated by some of the larger reports. For example, it will be desirable, even necessary, to run the programs that produce patron notices (such as notices for overdue or recalled items, or bills) on a nightly basis. However, some of the more detailed statistical reports, such as an analysis of total circulations by individual user categories within a given time period, may only need to be run infrequently (for instance, once a quarter) or by special request rather than on a regularly-scheduled basis.

The scheduling of batch-processed circulation operations may fall to the project manager, but most likely will be the responsibility of an individual within the organization who is able to weigh all the library system needs. if the library organization includes a staffed systems office, the head of that office would be the logical choice for this task.

STATISTICAL REPORTS OF CIRCULATION ACTIVITIES

Installing an automated circulation system provides libraries with more data on circulation activities than ever was available from a manual circulation system. Better yet, an automated system is capable of manipulating and packaging that data to suit a variety of management information needs, providing polished reports quickly and accurately. The data extracted from an automated circulation system will help library administrators make important collection-related decisions, assist library managers schedule staff to meet the anticipated workflow in circulation units, and both managers and administrators to identify heretofore unknown or unsuspected patterns of collection use. Although the system will provide a wealth of management information in these areas, remember that the provision of these statistics alone does not automatically improve the workplace for library staff or improve service to library users. It merely provides the means for analyzing library activities in a way that can lead to better working conditions for library staff and better service for library users.[4]

CIRCULATION FILES

In an automated circulation system, it is the file structure that makes it possible to collect and cumulate data on circulation activities. Basically, the system consists of three files: 1) *the current circulation file,* 2) *the circulation history file,* and 3) *the circulation abstract file.*

1. Current Circulation File

This file records all incomplete circulation transactions, in other words, current charges. When an item is discharged, the circulation transaction is considered to be complete, and the record is eliminated from this file.

2. Circulation History File

Once the circulation transaction is complete, e.g., the item has been discharged and the record purged from the current circulation file, that transaction is entered into the circulation history file. Depending on the system, the record may be entered into the circulation history file immediately, or may be part of a batch-processing program that the library activates according to a pre-determined schedule (e.g., daily, weekly, etc).

A circulation history file is essential to the system cumulating and reporting any kind of statistical information. Without the circulation history file, data would be lost each day as transactions were completed and eliminated from the current circulation file.

3. Circulation Abstract File

This file condenses the circulation history file and automatically performs any calculations that are routine to the system. After the data has been entered into the circulation abstract file, the system can extract any number of useful statistics for management reports.

SYSTEM-SUPPLIED STATISTICS AND REPORTS

An automated circulation system will provide circulation data for four broad areas: 1) use of the collection as defined by broad categories of library materials, 2) use of individual items owned by the library, 3) use of the collection as defined by library user groups, and 4) work loads and patterns of use within individual circulation units.

1. Information About Categories of Items Owned by the Library

Once information about the circulation or in-house use of individual items is recorded by automated circulation systems, this data can be compiled by the system for the purpose of determining collection use by meaningful collection development categories (i.e., by library location, item call number, etc.). An analysis of this type of data can be helpful in identifying what groups of items are or are not being used, which are being used more heavily than others, and which patron categories are using which groups of items. This information can be very useful in determining which areas of the collection need strengthening, and which, perhaps, could bear a decrease in collecting activity.

2. Information About Individual Items Owned by the Library

In addition to statistical data related to broad collection development categories, information can also be extracted from the system concerning the use of individual library items. Information detailing the number of times an individual item has been charged or used in-house, and the number of recalls or holds placed against an item at any one time can be supplied by the system. In addition, the system can provide an item-by-item listing of library materials that have been identified as missing or lost.

This item-specific data can be very useful in determining when additional copies of an item should be ordered to fill demand. It can also alert library staff to check heavily-used items for wear and tear and order additional copies if necessary. In addition, this information can help library staff determine when an item can be permanently removed from a the library collection or relocated to a remote storage area.

3. Information About Categories of Library Users

Data detailing circulation transactions by broad categories of library users or patron groups help pinpoint to what extent each group is using the library and with what frequency. Although many variables are considered when patron groups are defined earlier in the implementation process, it is also important to consider what categories will be meaningful for reporting library use statistics. By combining information about the circulation transactions of specific patron categories with information about general use of the collection, library managers may be able to predict future trends in collection usage. In addition, the identification of patron groups using the library infrequently or not at all helps identify where public relations efforts should be directed to increase use of the library. Identifying the degree of library use among patron groups can also be useful in planning new initiatives for library instruction.

In addition to generating data about the use of the library collection, analyzing the overdue, and bill and fine statistics by patron categories will help determine whether or not current loan policies are appropriate.[5]

4. Information About Work Loads in Circulation Units

Through the detailed data provided by the daily operations reports, as well as the overall circulation activity reported in the regularly-compiled summary reports (issued weekly, monthly or quarterly), managers within circulation units can better predict and plan for recurring workload cycles in their units. Staff can be scheduled more efficiently and effectively, achieving maximum utilization of limited resources. Staff within a single unit or among multiple units may be reallocated as a result of statistical information that proves a demonstrated need.

Reports detailing the data in the above four areas can be: 1) statistical reports that provide routine statistics, either summarized or in detail; 2) exception reports that point out areas that need attention; 3) on-demand reports that are produced irregularly at request and for a specific purpose; or 4) predictive reports that give comparisons to other data, such as a previous year's statistics in a given area, and allow predictions of future activity to be made.[6]

Within the routine statistical reports are the daily operations reports (see Fig. 12-1). These reports detail day-to-day activity within the automated circulation system, including any follow-up activities to which attention needs to be given, such as reminders to initiate searches for missing items, or begin withdrawal procedures for lost items. Produced by the system daily, these reports summarize by circulation service unit the following activities: charges, discharges, renewals, recalls, holds, in-house use of library materials, and any staff overrides of system policies. They can also pro-

```
┌─────────────────────────────────────────────────────────────────────────────┐
│  FIGURE 12-1   A sample of a Daily Operations Report                         │
├─────────────────────────────────────────────────────────────────────────────┤
│                                                                               │
│                                                                               │
│                         WALTER CIRCULATION Service Unit                       │
│      12/12/93                    Operations report                 Page   4   │
│                                                                               │
│      System overrides:                                                        │
│                                                                               │
│      Operator                       Terminal                                  │
│        ID      Date      Time        ID      Override                         │
│        TL1   12/10/93  10:38 AM     LHT1    expired ID 270 SA00 75 876Z A3     │
│        CJA   12/10/93  12:01 PM     JAC7    change discharge system date/time  │
│                                                 to 11/28/93 12:01 PM           │
│        CJA   12/10/93  12:02 PM     JAC7    change discharge system date/time  │
│                                                 to 11/28/93 12:01 PM           │
│        ZD1   12/10/93  01:56 PM     DZJA    blocked ID 210 SA01 92 123Z AI     │
│        TL1   12/10/93  02:52 PM     LHT1    policy table                       │
│                                                 Item record number ACF4772-001-0145 │
│                                                 Patron ID 210 SA01 23 713Z CW  │
│        TL1   12/10/93  02:52 PM     LHT1    policy table                       │
│                                                 Item record number ACF4771-001-0078 │
│                                                 Patron ID 210 SA01 23 713Z CW  │
│        TL1   12/10/93  02:52 PM     LHT1    policy table                       │
│                                                 Item record number ACF4771-001-0079 │
│                                                 Patron ID 210 SA01 23 713Z CW  │
│        TL1   12/10/93  02:52 PM     LHT1    policy table                       │
│                                                 Item record number ACF4776-001-0084 │
│                                                 Patron ID 210 SA01 23 713Z CW  │
│        TL1   12/10/93  02:52 PM     LHT1    policy table                       │
│                                                 Item record number ACF4776-001-0085 │
│                                                 Patron ID 210 SA01 23 713Z CW  │
│        TL1   12/10/93  02:53 PM     LHT1    policy table                       │
│                                                 Item record number ACF4776-001-0086 │
│                                                 Patron ID 210 SA01 23 713Z CW  │
│        ZD1   12/10/93  03:37 PM     DZJA    policy table                       │
│                                                 Item record number AEF2474-001-0002 │
│                                                 Patron ID 210 SA01 35 869Z BT  │
│        TL1   12/10/93  04:28 PM     LHT1    blocked ID 270 SA00 76 056Z AI     │
│        TL1   12/10/93  04:28 PM     LHT1    expired ID 270 SA00 76 056Z AI     │
│        ZD1   12/10/93  04:42 PM     DZJA    blocked ID 210 SA01 69 884Z AP     │
│        TL1   12/10/93  05:41 PM     LHT1    blocked ID 210 2296 87 864Z AA     │
│        ZD1   12/10/93  05:46 PM     DZJA    expired ID 210 SA01 26 481Z B4     │
│        TL1   12/10/93  10:53 PM     LHT1    renewals limit                     │
│                                                 Item record number ADQ5056-001-0002 │
│                                                 Patron ID 210 SA00 22 214Z C2  │
│                                                                               │
│      Override totals:                                                          │
│                                                                               │
│      System date/time for charges       0    Date due              0          │
│      System date/time for discharges    2    Policy table          7          │
│      Patron ID date   due date          0    Renewals limit        1          │
│                                                                               │
└─────────────────────────────────────────────────────────────────────────────┘
```

FIGURE 12-1 (continued)

```
                        WALTER CIRCULATION Service Unit
    12/12/93                   Operations report                    Page    5


    System activity totals:

    Charges                        305
    Discharges                     2125
    In-hand renewals               29
    Not-in-hand renewals           0
    Rush recalls placed            0
    Recalls placed                 23
    Holds placed                   0
    Combined recalls/holds placed  0
    Display items charged requests 0
    Print items charged requests   0




                        WALTER CIRCULATION Service Unit
    12/12/93                   Operations report                    Page    6


    Items with recall queue exceeding threshold:

    WALTER
      QA76.73;.B3 Z36 1993
      Zamora, Ramon.
        Visual basic for MS-DOS / Ramon Zamora, Don Inman, Bob Albrecht.
      Englewood Cliffs, N.J. : PTR Prentice Hall, c1993.
      Item record number ANL7470-001-0001
```

vide lists of newly-purchased items, items with recalls or hold queues that exceed system thresholds, overdue items, missing items for which staff need to initiate search procedures, and lost items for which staff need to initiate withdrawal and fines procedures. The daily operations reports enable circulation staff to monitor both circulation transactions and "housekeeping" activities in their specific unit.

The lists of overdue, missing or lost items provided by the daily operations reports allow library staff to track library materials more closely. Immediate notification by the system of exceptions to the smooth flow of library materials alerts staff that specific steps must be taken to ensure that library users have the most current information possible about a specific item. Especially useful are the "search" lists that the system generates (see Fig. 12-2). An item-by-item list of library materials missing from the shelves, these printouts are portable and can be used by library staff when physically searching for the item(s).[7]

SUPPLEMENTARY REPORTS

Probably no automated circulation system will provide all of the desired statistical summaries. Automated circulation systems have varied considerably in the number of additional statistical reports they have provided above and beyond the daily operations reports. Although automating circulation activities expands the potential to gather a wealth of statistical information, extracting that information from the system may not be possible without additional programming.

Numerous supplementary programs have been written for the express purpose of extracting statistics from automated circulation systems and compiling reports. Home-grown programs are being developed on a regular basis by systems staff or librarians who have an innate talent and interest in programming. Fortunately for other libraries without the staff or time to pursue additional programming, many of these library-developed programs are freely shared via system-specific user groups or listservs. These programs vary from the very basic to the very sophisticated, and cover many variations in reporting circulation or bill and fine statistics. However, since there are no standards or quality control governing the creation or distribution of these programs, library staff may find that adapting some of these programs is time-consuming and costly. The original program may have been written to work with a different version or release of the system software, or it may be incompatible with any in-house modifications the library has made to the vendor-supplied software. Rarely does a library simply install one of these shared programs. Depending on the modifications required prior to installation in another library, it may take as much programming time and effort to modify an existing program as it would to create an entirely new program.

Fortunately for libraries and their system programmers, many vendors are now offering supplementary report generating programs that work with the vendor-supplied system software and require minimal effort to install. These report generators require no knowledge of programming, but allow for considerable customization in producing reports.[8]

FIGURE 12-2   A sample "search" list generated by an automated circulation system

---

```
                              WALTER CIRCULATION
       12/12/93              Search for the following item(s):              Page   1

       WALTER
       BJ59 .B37 1993
       Barbour, Ian G.
          Ethics in an age of technology / Ian G. Barbour.  1st HarperCollins
       ed.  San Francisco, CA : HarperSanFrancisco, c1993.
       (The Gifford lectures ; 2nd ser., 1990-91)
       Item ID 3 1951 P00 237 780 W
       Charged to Missing (200 T000 00 0394 2N) on 12/10/93
       Searched 0 times before
       Search notes:




       WALTER
       LB2366.2 .A89 1991
       Astin, Alexander W.
          Assessment for excellence : the philosophy and practice of assessment
       and evaluation in higher education / Alexander W. Astin.  New York :
       American Council on Education : Macmillan ; Toronto : Collier Macmillan
       ; New York : Maxwell Macmillan, c1991.
       (The American Council on Education/Macmillan series on higher education)
       Item ID 3 1951 D00 563 267 1
       Charged to Lost (200 T000 00 0398 71) on 12/10/93
       Was charged to 200 T000 00 0671 7F
       Searched 0 times before
       Search notes:




       WALTER
       Quarto QA911 .H63x 1993 v.1
       Hoffmann, Klaus A.
          Computational fluid dynamics for engineers / Klaus A. Hoffmann, Steve
       T. Chiang.  Wichita, Kan. : Engineering Education System, c1993.
       Item ID 3 1951 P00 256 630 8
       Charged to Missing (200 T000 00 0394 2N) on 12/10/93
       Searched 0 times before
       Search notes:
```

REFERENCES

1. John Corbin, *Developing Computer-Based Library Systems* (Phoenix, AZ: Oryx Press, 1981): 104.
2. Ibid., pp. 104-5.
3. John Corbin, *Implementing the Automated Library System* (Phoenix, AZ: Oryx Press, 1988): 131.
4. Gary Carlson, "Circulation Systems on Microcomputer," *Drexel Library Quarterly* 20 (Fall 1984): 37.
5. Association of Research Libraries, Systems and Procedures Exchange Center, *Automated Circulation,* SPEC Kit #43 (Washington, D.C.: Association of Research Libraries, Office of Management Studies, Systems and Procedures Exchange Center, April 1978): 85-6.
6. Carol Pitts Hawks, "Management Information Gleaned from Automated Library Systems," *Information Technology and Libraries* 7 (June 1988): 131-3.
7. Ibid., p. 137.
8. Ibid., p. 132.

13 BEYOND IMPLEMENTATION

After the new automated circulation system has been implemented and staff are using it on a day-to-day basis, a true assessment can be made as to whether or not the system has fulfilled its potential and met the expectations of library staff and users. The period following the implementation of the system will be a time of discovery. The true capabilities and limitations of the system will become apparent, and the impact of the system will be felt throughout the organizational structure. It will also become clear that the system is dynamic rather than static, and requires on-going attention. Although anecdotal evidence will bring some of these issues to light, a formal evaluation of the new system by library staff and users allows a structured, systematic method for gathering detailed information about the performance and impact of the new system.

EVALUATING THE SYSTEM

It is easy to overlook the evaluation process once the new automated circulation system has become operational and the major portion of the implementation project has been completed. However, evaluating the new system should be considered an important part of the implementation project. It identifies hardware and software problem areas that need attention and provides yet another opportunity for fine-tuning policies and procedures developed to support the new system. In addition, requesting input on the system from library staff and users is a smart public relations gesture in that it encourages these individuals to establish a closer relationship with the library and its operations.

After the new automated circulation system has been implemented, both library staff and users should be allowed to evaluate the new system. Both groups should be surveyed with two goals in mind: 1) measurement of the success of the system, and 2) identification of any areas that could stand to be improved. Since the system will continue to evolve throughout its life in the library (via vendor-supplied and home-grown enhancements), regular surveys should be used to monitor this process. Regular feedback about the system from library staff and users provides a means for "taking the pulse" of the system to determine how useful it is and how well it fits the needs of the library and its users.[1] How regularly these surveys take place, or even when to conduct the first survey will depend on what time elapse will be most appropriate given the library's or the library's parent agency, institution, or organization's calendar (e.g., after the system has been operational one month, one quarter, one semester, one year, etc.).[2]

EVALUATIONS BY LIBRARY STAFF

When library staff are asked to evaluate the new system, they should be reviewing it in terms of its reliability (is there much or little downtime?), performance (does the system do the functions that were expected when the library initially purchased the system software?), and the response time (is it reasonable, or too slow?).[3] In addition, staff should be asked to compare the new system with the old system in terms of the functions performed, the management data provided, and the additional services or functions that are now possible.[4] Since most automated systems are intended to support day-to-day operations as well as to cumulate statistical information for library management, the ability of the system to effectively handle statistical report generation should also be included in any evaluation.[5]

Staff can also be asked to respond to a checklist of system requirements. Simply by checking "yes" or "no" by each item on the checklist, staff can indicate whether or not they are satisfied that the system has fulfilled each requirement.[6] Suggestion boxes, meetings with library staff, focus group sessions, and interviews with individual staff members are additional ways to receive feedback about the success of the system.

When conducting a staff evaluation of the system, no matter what technique or method is employed, it is important to make sure that the information collected most accurately represents how the system is actually performing on a day-to-day basis. To avoid any possible bias, seek input from staff other than those most closely aligned to the implementation project, such as systems office staff, the project manager or the project team.[7]

EVALUATIONS BY LIBRARY USERS

Evaluation of a new system by library users most often takes the form of printed surveys. Questions concerning circulation services under the new system are posed, and users respond by indicating their satisfaction with these services. A user survey could include questions such as the following:

Under the new system . . .
- Have circulation services improved with the implementation of the new circulation system?
- Have queues been reduced?
- Is the charge out process quicker and easier?
- Are records more accurate than they were in the old system, e.g., have you been erroneously fined or billed for late or non-returned items?
- Have your library experiences improved overall?

Although printed surveys are the easiest way to elicit this information from library users, interviews or focus groups are additional methods that may prove useful. Focus groups in particular may help the library pinpoint and gather detailed information about trouble areas.

In addition to mounting formal surveys, informal methods may also be used to collect information about library users' satisfaction with the new system. Informal methods can include gathering anecdotal information from library staff members as they interact with library users at service desks. This could include staff members' observations of increases or decreases in complaints or questions from library users about circulation functions, or increases or decreases in queues at service desks.[8]

SYSTEM EVALUATION OUTCOMES

A thorough evaluation of the new automated circulation system will probably identify some problems with the system or the policies or procedures developed to support the system. Some of these problems will be resolved quite easily. For instance, a problem with the system hardware might be solved by a slight modification of the system software, or shortcomings in the system software might be remedied by improving the hardware.[9] A procedural problem may be rectified by changing the way staff handle a particular task, or by adjusting the workflow in a specific unit.[10]

In addition to identifying problem areas that need correcting, the evaluation process also will highlight areas that may need fine-tuning. For instance, sending out notices to library users that announce that their charged items are coming due may be more effective than sending a series of overdue notices after the items become overdue.

Not all problems identified by the evaluation process will be as easily resolved. Some may require major revisions of the system software by the vendor, a solution that is rarely immediately available. For such long-term problems, it may be possible to provide short-term measures that make the problem bearable until the long-term solution is available. Most vendors are open to suggestions for future system corrections and enhancements, and the evaluation process is an excellent way to identify possible areas for future research and development by the vendor.

Staff and user expectations will be raised by the evaluation process; they will expect to see improvement in areas they have identified as problems. Whenever possible, corrective action should be taken as soon as possible for these problem areas.

UTOPIA VERSUS HARD REALITY

After the new automated circulation system has become operational and staff are using it to perform their daily tasks, a more realistic view of the capabilities and limitations of the new system will develop. Reality will replace conjecture. Although the specific details may vary from system to system, the following operational and organizational advantages and disadvantages can be expected to manifest themselves shortly after implementation (see Fig. 13-1).

THE OPERATIONAL ADVANTAGES OF AUTOMATION

The average circulation activity in an academic library equals approximately 0.4 times the number of volumes owned by the library. In a public library, circulation activity averages twice the number of volumes in the collection.[11] Add to this the large number of volumes used in-house, all of which must be processed if only to re-shelve them in their appropriate locations, and it's easy to see how circulation activities can create high-volume, labor-intensive workloads that outstrip the capabilities of most manual circulation systems. The situation worsens in larger libraries.

> Almost any manual circulation system begins to falter under an annual load of more than 250 thousand loans per year. The actual impact of this load on library staff is greater, amounting to more than 600 thousand transactions because each item lent must be discharged, and overdue notices must be sent out for at least 25 percent of all loans. In addition, records must be checked to determine the status of wanted materials not on the shelves.[12]

FIGURE 13-1

OPERATIONAL ADVANTAGES OF CIRCULATION AUTOMATION

1. Charge process is quicker and more efficient.
2. Routine, repetitive tasks are greatly reduced; some are eliminated entirely.
3. Accurate circulation information is available immediately online.
4. Inventory control is improved.
5. Delinquent library users are easier to track; sanctions are more easily impose.
6. Errors and misplaced items are less likely with online recall and hold functions.
7. New services may be implemented or existing services enhanced as automation frees staff time for other duties.
8. Management information improves; statistics can point to patterns that can be analyzed to improve collection development and staffing at service desks.

OPERATIONAL LIMITATIONS OF CIRCULATION AUTOMATION

1. Data must be entered into the system in machine-readable format; system will not always be able to identify data entry errors.
2. System is developed to handle routine situations; functions will not work as smoothly for non-routine, exceptional situations.
3. System will indicate with reasonable accuracy which items *are not* on library shelves, but the absence of tracking information will not indicate which items *are* on library shelves.
4. Statistical reports provided by the system may not meet all of the library's data needs.
5. System will require regular human intervention and regular maintenance to operate.
6. Short-term staffing needs and costs will increase during implementation of the system and creation of its databases.
7. Long-term staffing needs will most likely remain steady-state rather than decrease as staff time freed by automation is reallocated to previously-neglected activities.

It should come as no surprise that many of the benefits to automating circulation activities center on reducing the workload in these labor-intensive areas. Listed below are nine of these benefits, their fundamental relationship to the efficient, effective functioning of any library dramatically underscoring the inadequacies of manual or mechanical systems.

1. The Charge Process

Library staff and users both benefit from the efficiencies automation offers the charge process. The charge process becomes much quicker and more efficient with the elimination of the need to manually record information for each item charged. Once this tedious task is eliminated, queues at service desks are reduced and library users are able to conduct their business quickly. Library staff are freed from the busy-work involved in recording information in a manual system and are able to provide service to more library users in less time. Less stressed and frustrated by time constraints, staff find it easier to become more service-oriented, and increase their responsiveness to user needs and complaints.[13]

2. Routine, Repetitive Tasks

Inherent in circulation control are many repetitive record-keeping tasks that staff find boring. This boredom can decrease staff members' enthusiasm for their roles in the circulation process and contribute to a diminished accuracy of the files they are charged to create and maintain. Automation of circulation activities eliminates manual files and the need to maintain them, significantly reducing the clerical work associated with circulation control and the boredom such work inspires. It also frees up staff time for more interesting duties, and provides an opportunity to move staff from the back rooms of the circulation operation to the public forefront at service desks. Both library staff and users will benefit from an increase in the visibility and service potential of library staff.

3. Online Circulation Information

Libraries have functioned for many years, albeit not as efficiently or effectively as desired, with inaccurate, out-of-date information recorded in paper files. In libraries where the primary responsibility for creating and maintaining those files rests with student assistants with a high employment turnover rate, accuracy of circulation records has been a worthy goal not often achieved. Automating record-keeping functions removes the element of human error, dramatically improving the accuracy of circulation records and the overall integrity of the circulation files. The information contained in circulation records in an automated environment becomes more reliable.

In addition, an automated circulation system allows retrieval of individual circulation records via multiple access points; e.g., by the title, call number, or identification number of the charged item; or by the name or identification number of the library user. This eliminates the need to create and maintain duplicate records as is necessary in manual circulation files. Not only can circulation records be retrieve by multiple access points, but they can also be retrieved on demand. Data can also be reformatted quickly to meet a specific need, should the occasion arise.

4. Inventory Control

Automated inventory control means improved access to library materials for library users. An automated circulation system will track an item, wherever it may be, throughout the life of that item in the library. This includes the routine (e.g., charged to another patron) as well as the non-routine (e.g., at the bindery, missing, overdue).

5. Tracking Delinquent Library Users

An automated circulation system provides an automatic, cost-effective means for detecting overdue materials. Automating the fines process allows libraries to assess fines more consistently and uniformly for overdue items. Many libraries have found that automating the fines process has increased their success in collecting fines.[14] An automated circulation system offers a more effective way of handling delinquent users, providing the library with the means to impose sanctions (including revoking borrowing privileges) for the most notorious of delinquent users.

6. "Hold" and "Recall" Functions

The chance for error during the hold or recall processes (for instance, mistakenly charging an item recalled or on hold for one user to an entirely different user) decreases when these processes are automated. Once the hold or recall information is entered into the system, it automatically produces any needed notices and blocks any other individual from charging the item except the individual for whom the recall or hold was placed. The system will also automatically record and alert circulation staff to any expiration dates that occur during these processes. This reduces the number of items languishing for weeks or even months on circulation desk "hold" shelves, never picked up by the individuals requesting them.

7. Operating Costs

By turning over many of the formerly time-consuming clerical duties to the computer, staff time is freed up and can be diverted to other areas. The library can, without any additional staff, realize the potential to improve areas neglected prior to automation, or even offer new services. This by-product of automating circulation activities is critical in an era of decreasing budgets and increasing service demands.

8. Management Information

The statistics gathering and processing capabilities of automated circulation systems are a vast improvement over the minimal capabilities offered by manual systems where statistics are difficult if not impossible to extract. Information pertaining to the library collection, including evaluation of use in specific subject areas, support for acquisitions decisions, and identification of the need for multiple copies or weeding, are an improvement from the "gut feelings" often used to make these decisions in the absence of statistical data. Statistics detailing library use according to categories of library users are another attractive feature, and can detail which user groups are using which materials, or whether the loan periods are appropriate. Management data detailing overall circulation patterns and workloads may be helpful in determining what staffing configurations are needed in circulation units.

SPECIAL BENEFITS FOR SMALLER LIBRARIES

Although many libraries are small enough that their work loads do not overload their manual circulation systems, automating circulation activities provides other distinct benefits. Smaller libraries will find that automating circulation activities allows for a more efficient use of funds for circulation units through cost reduction or containment. Automation will also provide opportunities for improving and enhancing existing services. In addition, by capitalizing on the efficiencies offered by automated circulation systems, it is possible to expand the number and variety of user services offered by the library. Automated circulation systems provide the means to more efficiently deploy staff in circulation activities, perhaps allowing the library to enhance or expand library service without requiring additional staff. Finally, an automated circulation system offers the means for interfacing with other library systems, increasing the visibility of the library and its collections.

THE OPERATIONAL LIMITATIONS OF AUTOMATION

Like most things in this world, automated circulation systems are not infallible or perfect. In the balance, the benefits accrued by automating circulation activities outweigh the limitations; however, it is important to be aware of some of the shortfalls of automated circulation systems so no unpleasant surprises surface after the implementation of the new system.

The euphoria induced by some of the more dramatic improvements offered by the new system will be tempered with a dose of reality shortly after the system becomes operational. The benefits of automation can be forgotten quickly once staff realize that even computers cannot solve some of the age-old problems germane to circulation activities. For instance, a charge process that now takes only two to three seconds versus the one to two minutes it required in a manual system, will certainly reduce queues at service desks but will probably not eliminate them entirely.

Worse yet, staff will discover that the system will deliver an entirely new set of problems not encountered under the old system. For instance, batch-processed user notices may not reflect up-to-date information depending on whatever timelag there is between entering the information in the system and generating of the notices via batch programs. It is possible that incorrect information or invalid notices may be sent to users.

Although their enthusiasm for the system may be tempered somewhat by such unpleasant discoveries, informed, involved staff who have realistic expectations of the system will be able to cope with the limitations described below.

1. Information Processing

First, and foremost, the automated system will be unable to do anything unless information is fed into it in machine-readable form. There must be bibliographic and patron records in the system databases before any transactions can take place.

Once bibliographic and patron record data has been entered into system databases, the system takes that information at face value. Although the system can identify information that has been entered in an incorrect format or, on occasion, in the wrong field of a record, it will not be able to identify typographical errors or incorrect information, such as a misspelled name or incorrect address for a user. In addition, the system will be incapable of forming judgements about information included in its databases. It will not be able to intuit future situations based on past experiences with specific users or items.

2. Exceptional Situations

The system also will not deal well with exceptional situations. Automated circulation systems are developed to handle the routine (i.e., the majority of circulation transactions). Special procedures and system commands must be invoked to accommodate departures from routine.

3. Physical Limitations

The system can indicate whether or not a specific item is charged at any moment in time, but it cannot guarantee that an uncharged item is on the shelf. In-house use, thefts, and shelving errors are some of the activities that will remove items from their correct location on library shelves without any record of the removal appearing in the automated circulation system. Although data can be entered into the system recording in-house use or missing or lost items, there can be a significant timelag between when an item is removed from the shelf and when information about its removal is entered into the system. In the case of theft, this information often is not available until someone needs the item and attempts to locate it. The system can indicate if an item *is not* on the shelf, but it cannot always indicate if an item *is* on the shelf.

4. Statistical Reports

Statistics provided by the system will vary greatly from system to system, with some automated circulation systems providing only the most basic, rudimentary data. In a case such as this, it may be necessary to install additional software programs to generate the necessary statistical reports. Fortunately, this is not as large a problem as it once was. In addition to the availability of home-grown software programs that are shared among system user support groups, many vendors are now including supplemental report manager software with their automated circulation systems.

5. System Maintenance

The automated circulation system will not run itself. The system cannot be ignored after it has become operational; it will require human intervention for system operation and maintenance. In addition, as library and user needs change, the requirements for the automated circulation system will change. System parameters may need to be adjusted, or software modifications implemented. Vendor-supplied system fixes or new releases of the system software will need to be installed.

6. Short-Term Costs

In the short run, it will be expensive to automate circulation activities. The system will not be inexpensive to implement or operate, especially if the old and new circulation systems are run simultaneously for any length of time. Additional staff may be needed to handle the increased workload generated by running two systems side-by-side. Additional staff may also be required to create bibliographic and patron record databases and to enter existing circulation files into the new system. These increased staffing needs will be temporary, eventually disappearing when the old system and records are phased out and the new system becomes the sole source for circulation information. In addition, it may take time for staff to adjust to the new system and feel comfortable performing circulation functions on the system. Initially, it may take longer than expected to perform circulation activities on the system, especially those activities that are non-routine. However, after the old system is completely discontinued and routines on the new system have been established, these additional operational costs should decrease.

7. Long-Term Costs

One of the great myths surrounding the automation of circulation activities is that the new system will save the library great amounts of money by reducing the need for staff, even though the library literature is full of examples and warnings to the contrary. Realistically, the long-term costs of circulation activities will not reflect either a dramatic increase or decrease. Most likely, automating circulation activities will assist in maintaining a steady-state staffing level in circulation units, while helping circulation units avoid the regular staffing increases that manual circulation systems demand. Instead of reducing library budgets, automation of circulation activities allows libraries to more wisely and efficiently use the resources at their disposal. Although automating circulation activities does free up staff formerly committed to time-consuming, clerical tasks, most libraries have not found this additional staff time an expendable resource. Instead, they have re-directed this staff time toward areas previously neglected and long overdue for attention, or toward new services that were impractical or too costly under the old system.[15]

In addition to the initial purchase cost of the software and hardware needed to run the system, there will be expenses associated with the on-going operation and maintenance of the system.

These expenses will include: 1) computer time, staff and repairs necessary for the smooth operation of the system and functioning of the hardware; 2) supplies required to support system operations and functions, such as printer ribbons, printer paper, special forms, and bar codes; 3) staff and materials needed to support on-going training for library staff and users, including basic training for new staff or users and "refresher" or update sessions that convey system changes or enhancements; and 4) any on-going public relations activities.

The day-to-day, on-going operation of an automated circulation system is not cheap; however, the time-saving efficiencies provided by the system outweigh its operational expenses.[16]

THE ORGANIZATIONAL CHART

Much has been written about the impact automation has had on libraries. Traditional organizational structures have been examined in light of automation, and the morale and attitudes of library staff have been analyzed. Most authors agree that automating any library function engenders some degree of change, and that the maxim of "business as usual" is not applicable. Automation provides an opportunity for library administrators to examine traditional structures and revise them to meet changing needs. The results of a survey conducted in libraries where automated systems had been installed indicated that approximately three-quarters of those libraries had made organizational changes as a result of automation, including merging formerly separate departments.[17] Changes that are expected to improve the workplace for library staff will not only be accepted, but eagerly anticipated prior to their advent. Involving staff in the implementation project will make it easier for them to anticipate and accept the changes automation will bring.

One of the major changes engendered by the implementation of an automated circulation system is the decentralization of circulation files. The creation and maintenance of separate circulation files in each library unit is eliminated with the implementation of one large, common database for all to use. This shared database will contain more accurate, extensive information, resulting in better service to library users. A shared database also breaks down pre-automation barriers between circulation units, and between circulation units and other library departments.[18]

A shared database will blur the lines of responsibility for tasks traditionally considered the province of a specific library unit. Sharing the database as well as these tasks will often foster a cooperative spirit where previously none existed. For instance, the separation between circulation services and technical services will become less clear with the implementation of an automated circulation system. Staff in both circulation and technical services will create and modify system records, activities that were formerly the exclusive responsibility of technical services staff. By the same token, staff in both circulation and technical services will perform basic circulation functions (such as charge, discharge, recall, hold), activities that were formerly the exclusive responsibility of circulation staff. This breaking down of departmental barriers provides an opportunity to reconsider the library's organizational structure, especially if the existing structure has defined staff groups by function.

Accompanying the changes in the library's organizational chart will be changes in the way information is communicated throughout the library. Formal and informal communication lines will spring up as staff members discover how their actions or decisions will impact other library units accessing this centralized database. A formal committee that serves as a circulation advisory committee to library administration is a most effective way to coordinate formal communications, such as manuals, policy and procedure revisions, and standardized forms for reporting system problems or errors. Such an advisory group should include among its membership representation of the various library units utilizing the automated circulation system or its records.

STAFFING CIRCULATION UNITS

In two different surveys, one of GEAC installations and one of ARL libraries, the majority of respondents in both cases agreed that at best, staffing needs remained the same after automation, and at worst, increased.[19] The only area that has consistently demonstrated a decrease in staffing needed to support circulation functions in an automated environment is that centering on the preparation of overdue notices and bills.[20]

In some areas, staffing needs may increase sporadically and temporarily as a result of special projects or intermittent workloads. These short-term needs may be met with either temporary hires or short-term reallocation of existing staff. Prior to the system becoming operational, additional staffing may be needed to convert bibliographic records into the system's machine-readable format, as well as to barcode items on the library's shelves. If the library is not importing its patron database from another source, the library may need additional staff to "register" library users; e.g., to create patron records on the automated system and issue the requisite borrowing cards. After the system has been implemented, the library may still need staff to continue registering library users, creating online patron records and issuing borrowers' cards. After the initial registration rush during the implementation of the new automated circulation system, there will continue to be library users who will need online patron records and borrowers' cards. If these needs will be cyclical, for instance at the beginning of the new academic year in an academic or school library, additional staff may be needed to process borrowers cards at these peak times, depending on the size of the institution. The need to register library users on the online system will be intermittent, but on-going. Times of peak demand, when major efforts are required to create numerous new patron records, can be handled with staff temporarily hired for this purpose (if demand justifies this expense), or by temporarily diverting staff from an area with fewer pressing tasks.

In addition to temporary staffing, there are additional on-going roles that will need to be filled with staff hired specifically for these positions or by permanently re-assigning existing staff. One or more individuals will be needed to maintain the bibliographic and patron databases, and to ensure quality control as new data is entered. Data entry errors will occur and will need to be analyzed and corrected. Staff assigned this responsibility may be considered part of the library's system office if one exists.

Another area specific to automated circulation that will need on-going attention is the handling of print products produced by the system. The myriad assortment of print products produced by the system will need to be sent to one staff member or unit of the library for sorting and further distribution as appropriate. Daily operations reports will need to be sorted and sent to the appropriate service units, and user notices and bills will either need to be sent directly to library users or to the "owning" service unit for mailing. Staff freed by the automated system from processing patron notices and bills may be diverted to this activity.

Two additional tasks that will require additional staff effort, and perhaps additional staffing depending on how overburdened the current staff is, are on-going staff training and the upkeep of system documentation. Both of these tasks require a considerable amount of staff time, especially when system fixes or new releases of the system software are installed and revisions to the system documentation are needed. It is easy to overlook these activities or to mistakenly assume they will be taken care of when the need arises. If there will be no additional staff to handle these tasks, some thought needs to be given (before the system is implemented and the need arises) to how these two critical areas will be handled.

As job responsibilities change with the implementation of the automated circulation system, job descriptions will need to be rewritten to eliminate out-dated responsibilities and incorporate new ones. If skills, training or education to handle the new responsibilities differs from the old description, the job description will need to be revised accordingly.

Although circulation staff will not be sorry to see some of the more tedious circulation tasks (such as processing overdues, patron notices and bills) taken over by the new system, they will need to be given clear indications as to how this will impact their current assignment of responsibilities. The positive attributes of task reassignment, such as the variety that can now be added in place of formerly tedious tasks, should be emphasized. With job description revisions, as with every aspect of the implementation of the new system, staff who will be affected should be involved in the process as early as possible. Changes should be made as slowly as is practical in order to maintain a high level of staff productivity. "Old" jobs should evolve to the "new," naturally changing from one form to another, keeping the lines of communication open at every step of the way.[21]

THE END??

SYSTEM CHANGES

As mentioned previously, the new automated circulation system will not be a static system once it is operational, but will continue to be a dynamic, ever-changing system. A system that is constantly evolving means that portions of the original implementation project will never reach full closure. They will continue for the life of the system in the library.

Software, Procedure, or Policy Changes

Whenever system, procedural, or policy changes occur, some of the tasks that comprised the initial implementation project will need to be undertaken once again. The most frequent system changes are "fixes" that occur regularly (e.g., daily, weekly, or monthly, depending on the age and complexity of the system). Less frequent are the major system software revisions from the system vendor, with new releases of system software generally occurring at three to five year intervals.[22] System policies and procedures will undergo change as library and user needs change. At a minimum, documentation, training, and public relations will all need to be revisited as a result of these changes. Any new software release with major changes may require another major, comprehensive implementation project.

In addition, changes to system tables (if the system is table-driven), system display screens, and system functions all will require testing and debugging in a "test" database prior to implementation; publicity directed toward library staff and users will be needed to communicate the changes; and finally, a training program may need to be developed to deliver information to library staff and/or users about the new modification.

Hardware Changes

Automated systems and library budgets both change, providing libraries with opportunities to purchase additional system workstations, or upgrade or replace existing ones. As hardware changes are made, the library should be reviewing past decisions to see if they are still relevant in the new environment.[23] Again, tasks included in the major implementation project become relevant and must be repeated (e.g., wiring requirements for the new equipment must be determined, the new equipment must be tested prior to use, and staff training to operate the new equipment may need to be repeated).

CONTINUING EDUCATION: TRAINING, DOCUMENTATION AND PUBLICITY

It bears repeating that system training and revising system documentation are on-going tasks. Newly hired staff, existing staff who need refresher courses, and new system releases will all determine the need for on-going system training. System documentation will constantly be in need of revision as the system evolves and as the library's policies and procedures evolve with it. Finally, the public relations component will also require on-going attention so that any changes are communicated to library staff and users.

REFERENCES

1. Joseph R. Matthews, *Choosing An Automated Library System: A Planning Guide* (Chicago, IL: American Library Association, 1980): 76.
2. Judith E. Jeney, "Computers in Small Academic Libraries," *Catholic Library World* 60 (January-February 1989): 163.

3. John Corbin, *Implementing the Automated Library System* (Phoenix, AZ: Oryx Press, 1988): 142-6.

4. Jeney, "Computers in Small Academic Libraries," p. 163.

5. Carol Pitts Hawks, "Management Information Gleaned from Automated Library Systems," *Information Technology and Libraries* 7 (June 1988): 131.

6. John Corbin, *Developing Computer-Based Library Systems* (Phoenix, AZ: Oryx Press): 106.

7. Matthews, *Choosing An Automated Library System: A Planning Guide,* p. 75.

8. Ellen Hoffman, "Managing Automation: A Process, Not a Project," *Library Hi Tech* 6 (1988): 46.

9. Ibid.

10. Matthews, *Choosing An Automated Library System: A Planning Guide,* pp. 75-6.

11. James E. Rush Associates, inc., *Circulation Control,* vol. 2 of *Library System Evaluation Guide* (Columbus, OH: Rush Associates, 1983): 15.

12. Richard W. Boss and Judy McQueen, "Automated Circulation Control Systems," *Library Technology Reports* 18 (March/April 1982): 151.

13. James R. Martin, "Automation and the Service Attitudes of ARL Circulation Managers," *Journal of Library Automation* 14 (September 1981): 190-3.

14. Association of Research Libraries, Systems and Procedures Exchange Center, *Automated Circulation,* SPEC Kit #43 (Washington, D.C.: Association of Research Library, Office of Management Studies, Systems and Procedures Exchange Center, April 1978): 3.

15. Boss and McQueen, "Automated Circulation Control Systems," pp. 152-3.

16. Rush, *Circulation Control,* p. 16.

17. Danya Buck, "Bringing Up an Automated Circulation System: Staffing Needs," *Wilson Library Bulletin* 60 (March 1986): 31.

18. Corbin, *Implementing the Automated Library System,* p. 11.

19. See Buck, "Bringing Up an Automated Circulation System: Staffing Needs," p. 30; and Association of Research Libraries, Systems and Procedures Exchange Center, *Automated Circulation,* SPEC Kit #43, p. 3.

20. Matthews, *Choosing an Automated Library System: A Planning Guide,* p. 90.

21. Buck, "Bringing Up an Automated Circulation System: Staffing Needs," p. 31.

22. Hoffman, "Managing Automation: A Process, Not a Project," p. 48.

23. Ibid., p. 47.

14 CONCLUSION

The project to implement an automated circulation system may be overwhelming initially, however, the benefits to be realized by both library staff and library users are well-worth the considerable effort that will go into the project. No automated circulation system is perfect, nor will any system prove to be the panacea for all the library's woes. But implementing an automated circulation system will provide many opportunities for improving circulation activities, creating a more interesting workplace for library staff, and delivering better service to library users. The benefits to be realized from automating circulation activities will be more apparent at the conclusion of a well-planned implementation project that takes into account the unique needs of the library's staff and users and presents a realistic view of what the new system will offer. Although the major initiative to implement an automated circulation system may reach its conclusion once the new system is operational, many of the tasks associated with the original implementation project will not end the day the system becomes operational, but will last the lifetime of the system as changes occur.

This manual has advised the practitioner how to manage specific tasks that must be accomplished before implementing an automated circulation system. To close, some general practical tips that are not task-related, but which are very important nonetheless, are offered to the prospective project manager.

PRACTICAL TIPS FOR THE PROJECT MANAGER

The words of wisdom that follow are based on the experiences of former project managers. Although these practical tips will not make undertaking the implementation process entirely pain-free for the project manager, they will go a long way in reducing the discomfort factor of managing such a large, complicated project.

1. Plan, Plan, Plan
There is no one right way to manage a project entailing all the details that are included in the implementation of an automated circulation system. Many variables will need to be considered when tailoring the project to meet the needs of the library staff, library

users, and the system. What *is* important, however, is that there be a well-thought-out, comprehensive plan for implementing the new system. It is difficult to imagine the concept of too much planning being associated with a project of this magnitude.

There are techniques that can be used to assist with planning the implementation project, including the scheduling tools of the program evaluation and review technique (PERT) and the critical path method (CPM). Flowcharts also may be useful in identifying patterns of workflow in the old system and predicting workflow in the new system. Any of these techniques can be useful. The mechanics used to map a strategy for the implementation of the new system are not as critical as the fact that planning take place prior to beginning the implementation of the new system.

2. Coping With Delays

Expect individual task deadlines to change at least half-a-dozen times prior to the date on which the system finally will become operational. Delays are a given when automating any function, and certainly when automating a system incorporating such complex, inter-related variables as those found in automated circulation systems. Project participants, most especially the project manager, will encounter less stress if the deadlines have incorporated enough flexibility to cope with unexpected delays. Also, minimizing the impact these delays may have on subsequent project tasks will influence staff perception of the project's success.

However, even the best-laid plans go astray, to paraphrase a famous quote. A sound plan with plenty of flexibility to allow for deadline adjustment still may be subject to major, unexpected problems. Situations will arise that will wreak havoc on the most forgiving of schedules, and these situations will most likely be totally out of the control of the project manager. When this happens, the most the project manager can do is try to work with the source of the problem as much as is within her/his power, and, with the assistance of library administration, try and sort out the situation and resolve it with as little damage to the project as possible. Even this well-reasoned, controlled response will not always remedy a situation. There will be situations in which the project manager will receive no cooperation or support for resolving an issue, and the project may suffer some irreparable damage. For instance, the individual responsible for ordering the equipment for staff workstations may procrastinate beyond all hope of making the most flexible of deadlines. If that individual's superiors do not, for whatever reason, take control of the situation and effectively prod the individual or re-assign the responsibility, there is nothing more that the project manager can do beyond revising the plan to incorporate this delay. Once a project manager has done everything he or she can do to remedy a situation over which he or she has no control, the next step is to release any frustration generated by the situation and move on to other more manageable tasks. Fretting over situations that are not within the project manager's control add more stress to an already stressful position and may frustrate and demoralize that individual to the point of decreased effectiveness and productivity. The effects of stress are well-documented; the project manager should avoid, at all costs, adding to an already stressful role by fretting about a situation that is beyond her/his control.

3. Working with Project Participants

No automated system can be implemented by one lone individual. As stated earlier, part of the project manager's role is to act as a liaison and coordinator for the activities of the multitude of individuals and groups who will be involved in the implementation of the new automated circulation system. As long as the project manager is dependent on other individuals to assume responsibility for the completion of certain tasks such as drafting a procedure for the circulation manual, ordering the system hardware, writing supplemental software programs, or wiring for electricity or telecommunications, the project manager is at the mercy of those individuals' schedules and personality characteristics, either of which may impact how the project proceeds. An absolute given is that at least one individual involved in the project will be a serious procrastinator, and another will have an impossible schedule. The degree of flexibility within the project schedule will determine how easily these differences are accommodated, and will also determine whether or not the project participants will be speaking to one another at the conclusion of the project. A flexible schedule will go a long way to accommodate all the individuals involved in the project and will help foster a more cooperative spirit.

The project manager will need to be aware of the strengths and weaknesses individual participants will bring to the project, especially within the group of individuals comprising the project team. If one individual has difficulty grasping the finer technical points of the system but is a gifted public speaker, don't assign that individual to assist in testing all the vagaries of the system. That individual will be happier and more productive as part of the core group that will conduct training sessions. Channeling individuals toward tasks that capitalize on their strengths will allow them to complete their assignments quickly and accurately. Also, by assigning tasks that individuals can complete successfully, morale and productivity remain high among project participants. Conversely, thrusting individuals into ill-fitting roles creates an unhappy, unproductive atmosphere where every task is a chore, and one's best efforts are never enough. Everyone has areas in which they excel—make the most of the diverse array of skills and talents to be found among the project's participants.

4. Representing the System

The project manager will be responsible for representing the new system as positively and accurately as possible. It is critical that system strengths be emphasized in public, rather than dwelling on its weaknesses. This is not to say that the system's shortcomings should not be identified and addressed, but that they should be dealt with matter-of-factly and constructively. When talking informally with library staff, addressing trainees during a training session, or formally delivering written or verbal reports on the progress of the implementation project, it is essential that the project manager and members of the project team represent the system in the most positive light possible. Library staff for whom the system is still an unknown, and possibly a frightening unknown, should not have their ultimate acceptance of the system jeopardized by pessimists or nay-sayers from the core implementation project group.

5. Maintaining a Sense of Humor

At all times, in all situations, the project manager must maintain a sense of humor. Humor is one of the most effective means for alleviating stress. Humor is also beneficial in diffusing potentially unpleasant situations. An individual who sees the humor in a situation releases the frustration and fear it may generate by articulating the absurdities of the situation to another. Laughter is, indeed, the best medicine.

6. Maintaining a Sense of Perspective

In addition to a sense of humor, a sense of perspective is effective for reducing stress. A favorite ploy for maintaining one's perspective is to place the situation in the distant future and weigh its relative importance; e.g., five years from now, will it really matter that the barcoding project was 80% instead of 100% complete when the system was activated? Bear in mind that no matter how difficult or unpleasant a current situation may be, eventually it will come to an end. Although some days it will seem as though the implementation project will never reach its goal of system activation, eventually it *will* happen.

7. Learning From Experience

Even if the project manager has planned for every possible situation, achieved a satisfactory working relationship with project participants, maintained a sense of humor, and placed stressful situations in a perspective that helps diminish their severity, uncomfortable situations will still be unavoidable. If the project manager has dealt with a situation in an appropriate fashion, yet it defies a logical resolution, the situation should be considered a learning experience. Rare indeed, is the situation from which an individual cannot extract some valuable experience for future use. There is always something to be learned in any situation, and, fortunately for those managers who are always trying to improve their management skills, the opportunity for learning new skills never ends.

ONE FINAL WORD

The successful project manager will reach the end of a thoroughly-planned, comprehensive implementation project with her or his perspective, sense of humor, and sanity intact. The individual who is able to roll with the punches will find, a year later, that most of the frustration and headaches associated with the implementation project are a distant memory. Instead, the strongest impression remaining will be a sense of pride in a job well done, and the overwhelming pleasure that results from seeing an automated circulation system that has become firmly and happily woven into the fabric of normal library operations.

BIBLIOGRAPHY

Annual Review of Information Science and Technology. Washington, D.C.: American Society for Information Science, v. 1- , 1966- .

Association of Research Libraries, Systems and Procedures Exchange Center. *Automated Circulation,* SPEC Kit #43, April 1978. Washington, D.C.: Association of Research Libraries, Office of Management Studies, Systems and Procedures Exchange Center, 1978.

Association of Research Libraries, Systems and Procedures Exchange Center. *Automated Library Systems in ARL Libraries,* SPEC Kit #126, July-August, 1986. Washington, D.C.: Association of Research Libraries, Office of Management Studies, Systems and Procedures Exchange Center, 1986.

Association of Research Libraries, Systems and Procedures Exchange Center. *Barcoding of Collections in ARL Libraries,* SPEC Kit #124, May 1986. Washington, D.C.: Association of Research Libraries, Office of Management Studies, Systems and Procedures Exchange Center, 1986.

Bahr, Alice Harrison. *Automated Library Circulation Systems 1979-80.* White Plains, NY: Knowledge Industry Publications, 1979.

Barkalow, Pat. "Conversion of Files for Circulation Control," *Journal of Library Automation,* v. 12, September 1979, pp. 209-13.

Boss, Richard W. "Circulation Systems: The Options," *Library Technology Reports,* v. 15, January/February 1979, pp. 7-105.

Boss, Richard W. "General Trends in Implementation of Automated Circulation Systems," *Journal of Library Automation,* v. 12, September 1979, pp. 198-202.

Boss, Richard W. *The Library Manager's Guide to Automation.* White Plains, NY: Knowledge Industry Publications, Inc., 1979.

Boss, Richard W. *The Library Manager's Guide to Automation,* Third Edition. Boston, MA: G. K. Hall & Co, 1990.

Boss, Richard W. and Judy McQueen. "Automated Circulation Control Systems," *Library Technology Reports,* v. 18, March/April 1982, pp. 125-266.

Bruer, J. Michael. "The Public Relations Component of Circulation System Implementation," *Journal of Library Automation,* v. 12, September 1979, pp. 214-18.

Buck, Dayna. "Bringing Up an Automated Circulation System: Staffing Needs," *Wilson Library Bulletin,* v. 60, March 1986, pp. 28-31.

Carlson, Gary. "Circulation Systems on Microcomputers," *Drexel Library Quarterly,* v. 20, Fall 1984, pp. 34-47.

Cohn, John M., Ann L. Kelsey and Keith Michael Fiels. *Planning for Automation: A How-To-Do-It Manual for Librarians,* How-To-Do-It Manuals for Librarians, no. 25. New York, NY: Neal-Schuman Publishers, Inc., 1992.

Corbin, John. *Developing Computer-Based Library Systems.* Phoenix, AZ: Oryx Press, 1981.

Corbin, John. *Directory of Automated Library Systems.* New York, NY: Neal-Schuman Publishers, 1989.

Corbin, John. *Implementing the Automated Library System.* Phoenix, AZ: Oryx Press, 1988.

Corbin, John. *Managing the Library Automation Project.* Phoenix, AZ: Oryx Press, 1985.

Duval, Beverly K. and Linda Main. *Automated Library Systems.* Westport, CT: Meckler Publishing, 1992.

Fairfax County Public Library. *Training Checklist for Circulation Staff.* Fairfax, VA: The Library, 1985.

Fayen, E. G. "Automated Circulation Systems for Large Libraries," *Library Technology Reports,* v. 22, July/August 1986, pp. 385-473.

Fouty, Kathleen. "Online Patron Records and Privacy: Service vs. Security," *Journal of Academic Librarianship,* v. 19, November 1993, pp. 289-93.

Freedman, Maurice J. "Automation and the Future of Technical Services," *Library Journal,* v. 109, June 15, 1984, pp. 1197-1203.

Frohmberg, Katherine A. and William A. Moffet. *Research on the Impact of a Computerized Circulation System on the Performance of a Large College Library. Final Report.* ERIC Document Reproduction no. ED 235 806.

Garcia, C. Rebecca and Frank R. Bridge. *Small Libraries Online: Automating Circulation and Public Access Catalogs. Participant Workbook* (1989). ERIC Document Reproduction no. ED 326 246.

Getz, Malcolm. "More Benefits of Automation," *College and Research Libraries,* v. 49, November 1988, pp. 534-44.

Hawks, Carol Pitts. "Management Information Gleaned from Automated Library Systems," *Information Technology and Libraries,* v. 7, June 1988, pp. 131-38.

Hoffmann, Ellen. "Managing Automation: A Process, Not a Project," *Library Hi Tech* v. 6, 1988, pp. 45-54.

Intner, Sheila. "Microcomputer Backup to Online Circulation," *Journal of Library Automation,* v. 14, December 1981, pp. 297-99.

Jeney, Judith E. "Computers in Small Academic Libraries," *Catholic Library World,* v. 60, January-February 1989, pp. 160-63, 176.

Jestes, Edward C. "Manual Versus Automated Circulation: A Comparison of Operating Costs In A University Library," *Journal of Academic Librarianship,* v. 6, July 1980, pp. 144-50.

Juergens, Bonnie. "Staff Training Aspects of Circulation System Implementation," *Journal of Library Automation,* v. 12, September 1979, pp. 203-8.

Leggate, Peter and Hilary Dyer. "The Microcomputer in the Library: V. Circulation Control and Serials Control," *Electronic Library,* v. 4, August 1986, pp. 218-29.

Library Circulation Systems and Automation: A Select Bibliography. Josephine Crawford, ed. Chicago, IL: American Library Association, 1989.

McDonald, David R. "Libraries and Computing Centers: Issues of Mutual Concern; The Ingredients of a Good Relationship: The Library's Point of View," *Journal of Academic Librarianship,* v. 13, January 1988, pp. 364a-64b.

Martin, James R. "Automation and the Service Attitudes of ARL Circulation Managers," *Journal of Library Automation,* v. 14, September 1981, pp. 190-94.

Matthews, Joseph R. "The Automated Circulation System Marketplace: Active and Heating Up," *Library Journal,* v. 107, February 1, 1982, pp. 233-35.

Matthews, Joseph R. "The Automated Library System Marketplace, 1982: Change and More Change!" *Library Journal,* v. 108, March 15, 1983, pp. 547-53.

Matthews, Joseph R. *Choosing an Automated Library System: A Planning Guide.* Chicago, IL: American Library Association, 1980.

Matthews, Joseph R. *Guidelines for Selecting Automated Systems.* Chicago, IL: American Library Association, Library and Information Technology Association, 1986.

Matthews, Joseph R. "Microcomputer Circulation Control Systems: An Assessment," *Library Technology Reports,* v. 22, January/February 1986, pp. 5-152.

Matthews, Joseph R. *A Reader on Choosing an Automated Library System.* Chicago, IL: American Library Association, 1983.

Matthews, Joseph R. "20 Qs & As on Automated Integrated Library Systems," *American Libraries,* v. 13, June 1982, pp. 367-71.

Matthews, Joseph R. and Kevin Hegarty. *Automated Circulation: An Examination of Choices.* Chicago, IL: American Library Association, 1984.

Metz, Paul. "Circulation Systems: The Tinker Toys of Library Automation?" *Journal of Academic Librarianship,* v. 13, January 1988, pp. 364c-64d.

Nelson, Bonnie R. "Implementation of On-line Circulation at New York University," *Journal of Library Automation,* v. 12, September 1979, pp. 219-32.

Potter, William G. "Library Automation: Hitting the Links," *Journal of Academic Librarianship,* v. 14, May 1988, pp. 102a-102d.

Rahn, Erwin. "Bar Codes for Libraries," *Library Hi Tech* v. 2, 1984, pp. 73-77.

Rush, James E. *Circulation Control,* vol. 2 of *Library System Evaluation Guide.* Columbus, OH: Rush Associates, 1983.

Saffady, William. "Library Automation: An Overview," *Library Trends,* v. 37, Winter 1989, pp. 269-81.

Schottlaender, Brian. *Retrospective Conversion: History, Approaches, Considerations.* New York, NY: Haworth Press, 1992.

Shaw, Debora. "Staff Opinions in Library Automation Planning: A Case Study," *Special Libraries,* v. 77, Summer 1986, pp. 140-51.

Stockey, Edward A. "The Design of a Backup for an Online Circulation System at Indiana State University," *Library Hi Tech News* n. 46, February 1988, pp. 1-4.

Tracy, Joan. "Automated Circulation of Unbound Periodicals: A Survey of Practices," *Library Hi Tech,* v. 1, Winter 1983, pp. 68-78.

INDEX